# TREES
*for*
# TENNESSEE

# TREES

*for*

# TENNESSEE

## Judy Lowe

COOL
SPRINGS
PRESS

Nashville, Tennessee
A Division of Thomas Nelson, Inc.
www.ThomasNelson.com

Published by Cool Springs Press, a Division of Thomas Nelson, Inc., P.O. Box 141000, Nashville, Tennessee, 37214.

First printing 2004
Printed in the United States of America
10 9 8 7 6 5 4 3 2 1

Managing Editor: Mary Morgan
Horticulture Editor: Michael Wenzel, Atlanta Botanical Garden
Copyeditor: Michelle Adkerson
Designer: Bill Kersey, Kersey Graphics
Production Artist: S.E. Anderson

On the cover: Gingko, photographed by Liz Ball

We gratefully acknowledge the contributions of the following authors who have granted their permission to use selected entries:
American Hornbeam (pg. 14) and Black Gum (pg. 18)—James A. Fizzell; Black Gum (pg.18) and Norway Spruce (pg. 64)—Ralph Snodsmith; Blue Atlas Cedar (pg. 20), Thornless Honey Locust (pg. 100), and Winter King Hawthorn (pg. 106)—Liz Ball; Chinese Pistachio (pg. 28), Flowering Crabapple (pg. 36), Purple Leaf Plum (pg. 74), and Sweet Bay Magnolia (pg. 96)—Dale Groom; Black Gum (pg. 18), Cornelian Cherry (pg. 30), and Norway Spruce (pg. 64)—Tim Boland, Laura Coit, and Marty Hair; Dawn Redwood (pg. 32), Flowering Crabapple (pg. 36), Kousa Dogwood (pg. 56), Kwanzan Cherry (pg. 58), and Yoshino Cherry (pg. 110)—Walter Reeves and Erica Glasener; Deodar Cedar (pg. 34), Red Oak (pg. 80), Sugar Maple (pg. 94), and Willow Oak (pg. 104)—Toby Bost; Japanese Stewartia (pg. 50), Katsura Tree (pg. 54), and Leyland Cypress (pg. 62)—Andre Viette and Jacqueline Heriteau

Visit the Thomas Nelson website at www.ThomasNelson.com

# Table *of* Contents

How To Use This Book . . . . . . . . . . . . . . . . . . . . .7

50 Great Trees for Tennessee . . . . . . . . . .9–111

American Holly 12
American
   Hornbeam 14
Bald Cypress 16
Black Gum 18
Blue Atlas Cedar 20
Canadian Hemlock 22
Carolina Silverbell 24
Chaste Tree 26
Chinese Pistachio 28
Cornelian Cherry 30
Dawn Redwood 32
Deodar Cedar 34
Flowering
   Crabapple 36
Flowering
   Dogwood 38
Fringe Tree 40
Ginkgo 42
Golden Rain Tree 44

Japanese
   Cryptomeria 46
Japanese Maple 48
Japanese
   Stewartia 50
Japanese Zelkova 52
Katsura Tree 54
Kousa Dogwood 56
Kwanzan Cherry 58
Lacebark Elm 60
Leyland Cypress 62
Norway Spruce 64
Ornamental Pear 66
Paperbark Maple 68
Persian Ironwood 70
Pin Oak 72
Purple Leaf Plum 74
Redbud 76
Red Maple 78
Red Oak 80

River Birch 82
Sassafras 84
Saucer Magnolia 86
Serviceberry 88
Sourwood 90
Southern Magnolia 92
Sugar Maple 94
Sweet Bay
   Magnolia 96
Sweet Gum 98
Thornless Honey
   Locust 100
Tulip Poplar 102
Willow Oak 104
Winter King
   Hawthorn 106
Yellowwood 108
Yoshino Cherry 110

Gardening Basics . . . . . . . . . . . . . . . . . . . . . . . .112

Glossary . . . . . . . . . . . . . . . . . . . . . . . . . . . . . .120

Bibliography . . . . . . . . . . . . . . . . . . . . . . . . . . .124

Photography Credits . . . . . . . . . . . . . . . . . . . . .124

Plant Index . . . . . . . . . . . . . . . . . . . . . . . . . . . .125

# How To Use This Book

Each entry in this guide provides you with information about a plant's particular characteristics, habits, and basic requirements for active growth as well as my personal experience and knowledge of the plant. I include the information you need to help you realize each plant's potential. Only when a plant performs at its best can one appreciate it fully. You will find such pertinent information as mature height and spread, bloom period and colors (if any), sun and soil preferences, water requirements, fertilizing needs, pruning and care, and pest information.

## Sun Preferences

Symbols represent the range of sunlight suitable for each plant. Some plants can be grown in more than one range of sun, so you will sometimes see more than one sun symbol.

**Full Sun**     **Part Sun/Shade**     **Full Shade**

## Additional Benefits

Many plants offer benefits that further enhance their appeal. The following symbols indicate some of the more important additional benefits:

 **Attracts Butterflies**

 **Attracts Hummingbirds**

 **Produces Edible Fruit**

 **Has Fragrance**

 **Produces Food for Birds and Wildlife**

 **Drought Resistant**

 **Suitable for Cut Flowers or Arrangements**

 **Long Bloom Period**

 **Native Plant**

 **Supports Bees**

 **Good Fall Color**

 **Provides Shelter for Birds**

## Complementary Plants

For many of the entries, I provide landscape design ideas as well as suggestions for companion plants to help you achieve striking and personal gardening results from your garden. This is where I find the most enjoyment from gardening.

## Recommended Selections

This section describes specific cultivars or varieties that I have found particularly noteworthy. Give them a try.

# 50 Great Trees *for* Tennessee

Try to imagine a world without trees—without clouds of white dogwoods in spring, without the stately shade trees that sheltered you and the games of your childhood, without pecans or pine cones, without the brilliant orange, scarlet, and yellow foliage that send us into colder weather.

No wonder planting a tree is the first yard chore for people with a new home. Trees give your property and neighborhood character. They save energy dollars, provide shade and screening, and solve other landscaping problems. And of course, they're good for the environment.

## Start with a Few Questions

To find the best tree for your yard, ask yourself a few questions first. What is your ultimate goal for this tree? What purpose will it serve in your landscape? Do you want shade? Flowers in spring? A tree that will attract birds to your yard? Colorful fall foliage? A buffer between you, your neighbors, and the outside world? A tree that will be interesting to look at in more than one season?

Dogwoods, for instance, flower in spring, have leaves that turn fiery in fall, and also produce berries that attract a host of feathered friends.

Do you want a deciduous tree—one that drops its leaves in fall—such as a maple; a broadleaf evergreen, such as a southern magnolia; or a needled evergreen, such as a Canadian hemlock? A deciduous tree means raking leaves. But it also means you can position the tree to block the

Heritage River Birch

sun from reaching your house in summer to decrease air-conditioning costs, but let the sun through in winter to help warm the house.

Evergreens block the sun in summer and winter. They're mostly used to add a green touch to the yard in cold weather, when everything else looks brown. They also work well as a year-round screen to hide unsightly views. Evergreens tend to grow more slowly than deciduous trees, which may be helpful or not, depending on your goals for the tree. Although evergreens never lose all their leaves or needles, they do shed some of them each year.

## The Homeowner's Biggest Mistake

How large will that big tree grow? Not learning the answer to that question—*before* buying and planting—is probably the biggest mistake homeowners make when choosing trees. If you don't know the mature size of the tree you're planting, you're all too likely to place it too close to your house, the sidewalk, or the street. With one-story homes especially, keep perspective firmly in mind. Ask yourself how, when the tree matures, its size and the size of your house will compare. Also look up—are there power lines that the tree may interfere with when it reaches mature size? And where will its branches be in relation to your roof?

## Landscape Harmony

What shape or form will the tree develop as it grows? Will it be very narrow, like a column, or pyramidal or weeping? Look at photos of the tree at maturity to be sure. Think of the effect each form will have not

Maples in Fall Color

Japanese Zelkova

only by itself, but in relation to surrounding plantings, other trees in the yard, and structures such as the house, garage, or fence. While a weeping ornamental cherry is a delight in spring and a good accent shape, you wouldn't want to fill your yard with all weeping trees. That would dilute the effect.

## The "Perfect" Tree

Does the tree you're considering develop any messy fruits, seeds, or droppings? A sweet gum is a pleasure in fall because of its scarlet leaves, but it's a nuisance in spring when the "balls" keep fouling up the lawn mower. And the hard, brown leaves of a southern magnolia aren't easy to deal with.

That doesn't mean you have to give up on trees with messy habits. Instead, site them so their liability isn't a drawback. Put that magnolia in a mulched bed instead of the lawn, and the dropped leaves won't be nearly so noticeable. Or plant the sweet gum at the fringe of the woods, so the balls can fall harmlessly to the ground without causing a problem. Or try planting messy trees in the center of a ground-cover bed.

It's almost impossible to imagine a beautiful landscape without trees. Not only do they increase the value of your property, they add a sense of permanence and comfort. In the following pages, you'll find the perfect tree for any spot in your yard.

# American Holly
*Ilex opaca*

### *A Splash of Green in the Coldest Weather Plus Bright-Red Berries*

Not all the trees you plant in your yard should be shade trees or flowering trees. Everyone needs at least one evergreen to add a touch of green to the landscape during the cold, dreary months of winter. And what better choice than the native American holly? Just in time for the holidays—that season of red and green—it produces bright-crimson berries, providing a naturally decorated tree for your yard.

## Top Reasons to Plant

- ○ Green in the winter
- ○ Bright-red berries
- ○ Good for cutting during winter holidays
- ○ Effective screen
- ○ Few bothersome insects or diseases
- ○ Attractive from indoors in winter

## Useful Hint

December is the ideal time to cut holly sprigs and branches to use indoors.

## Bloom Color
White blooms followed by red berries

## Bloom Period
Blooms in spring with berries in fall and winter

## Height/Width
15 to 40 feet x 8 to 30 feet

## Planting Location
- Moist, well-drained, acidic soil
- Full sun or mostly sun

## Planting
- Select a spot that isn't windy.
- For every three to six female hollies, which produce the berries, plant a male that blooms at the same time for pollination—the males and females can be up to 100 feet apart.
- Plant in spring.
- Dig the hole as deep as the rootball and twice as wide.
- Place the tree in the hole and fill in with soil dug from the hole.
- Water well.
- Mulch well.

## Watering
- Water when rainfall is less than an inch weekly.

## Fertilizing
- In early years, fertilize at the end of March or in April using an organic fertilizer such as Holly-tone®.

## Suggestions for Vigorous Growth
- Prune anytime to maintain the pyramidal shape.

# Easy Tip

Place American holly where it can be seen from the street and especially from indoors in winter.

## Pest Control
- Holly leafminers may appear—they leave "trails" in the leaves but generally aren't harmful.
- Scale is sometimes a problem—it looks like tiny brown bumps on the stems and undersides of leaves.
- Spittlebugs, which can be recognized by the foam they leave behind, may be a problem.
- If any of these are serious infestations, consult the Extension Service about controls.

## Complementary Plants
- Use several American hollies together for screening or a windbreak.

## Recommended Selections
- 'Jersey Princess' has lustrous dark-green leaves ('Jersey Knight' is the male pollinator).
- Hybrid hollies such as 'Fosteri', 'Nellie R. Stevens', and especially 'Emily Bruner' and 'James Swan', which were discovered in Knoxville, are proven performers.

# American Hornbeam

*Carpinus caroliniana*

*A Tough Native Tree That Tolerates a Variety of Conditions*

An interesting smaller tree, American hornbeam is a tough native of the bottomlands. It tolerates wet or dry, acid or alkaline soils, sunny or shaded situations. Hornbeam has attractions in all seasons. The catkins are light-green as leaves begin to open. The leaves are small enough to allow the interesting structure of the tree to show through. Fall color is yellow to orange. And in winter, the beautiful smooth, gray bark on multiple, muscular trunks is quite handsome.

## Top Reasons to Plant

○ Four seasons of interest
○ Grows well under the shade of larger trees
○ Good fall color
○ Muscular structure
○ Smooth, gray bark attractive in winter
○ Relatively small
○ Few bothersome insects and diseases
○ Good shelter for birds

## Useful Hint

Put American hornbeam where you can appreciate its interesting four-season character.

**Bloom Color**
Light-green

**Bloom Period**
Spring

**Height/Width**
20 feet x 20 feet

**Planting Location**
- Prefers moist, well-drained soil, but tolerates alkalinity and other difficult situations
- Sun to partial shade

**Planting**
- Transplant balled-and-burlapped trees when they are small.
- Plant in spring.
- Site no closer than 10 feet to a structure.
- Dig the hole a little shallower than the rootball and twice as wide.
- Set the tree in the hole, and remove the burlap.
- Fill the hole with original soil.
- Water well.
- Use any remaining soil to make a saucer around the tree.

**Watering**
- Water during extended dry periods.

*Easy Tip*

American hornbeam is especially useful in a site where larger, overhanging trees cast shade and keep the soil moist.

**Fertilizing**
- No fertilizer is needed.

**Suggestions for Vigorous Growth**
- Prune if you prefer, but American hornbeam seldom needs it.

**Pest Control**
- No serious pests or diseases trouble this tree.

**Complementary Plants**
- American hornbeam works best as a specimen tree.

**Recommended Selections**
- Plant the native species.

# Bald Cypress
*Taxodium distichum*

## A Native with Needles That Change Color in Autumn

Most of us are used to thinking of trees that have needles as evergreen and of trees that have leaves as deciduous (losing their foliage in fall). Bald cypress completely upsets those beliefs—it's a tree with needles, but they become a wonderful cinnamon color in autumn and then fall off. Trees like this are called deciduous conifers—they bear cones, like evergreens, but the needles fall in winter, like most trees with leaves.

## Top Reasons to Plant

- Beautiful shedding bark
- Tolerates most soils
- Good cover for birds
- Pleasant fragrance
- Few insects and diseases
- Lovely fall color

## Useful Hint

Place this tree where its shedding bark can be admired.

16

## Bloom Color
Purplish drooping clusters

## Bloom Period
Early spring

## Height/Width
50 to 85 feet x 18 to 65 feet

## Planting Location
- Ideal for boggy, acidic soil but tolerates almost any type of soil that isn't alkaline
- Sun

## Planting
- Plant in early fall or in spring.
- Allow plenty of space—this tree grows very large.
- Dig the hole the same depth as the rootball and twice as wide.
- Place the tree in the hole and fill in with soil dug from the hole.
- Mulch well, keeping mulch 2 inches away from trunk.

## Watering
- Water weekly for the first two years if there isn't adequate rainfall.
- After two years, no additional watering is needed.

## Fertilizing
- During the first few years, fertilize each fall after the needles have fallen; use a high-nitrogen fertilizer according to package directions.

## Easy Tip
Bald cypress thrives in that permanently wet spot in the yard, but it also does well with average moisture.

## Suggestions for Vigorous Growth
- Yellowing needles probably indicate soil that's not acidic enough—spray with chelated iron and use fertilizer for acid-loving plants.
- Don't worry about knobby growths at the base; these "knees" are normal in wet sites.
- Prune dead branches anytime.

## Pest Control
- If bagworms appear, pick them off at dusk.
- Spray the tree with water if spider mites cause the needles to turn brown anytime except fall.

## Complementary Plants
- This large tree works best as a specimen.

## Recommended Selections
- 'Apache Chief' is a handsome, wide-spreading tree.

# Black Gum
*Nyssa sylvatica*

## A Beautiful Native with Fine Fall Foliage

One of our finest native trees, black gum has a distinctive pyramidal form, good branching, and excellent fall color. It consistently provides a fall display of brilliant scarlet, yellow, orange, and purple leaves. In summer, it has lustrous, shiny green foliage. While it prefers swampy places, black gum is found growing in upland sites, woodlots, and abandoned farmlands. Its fruits, about the size of cherries, attract birds.

## Top Reasons to Plant

○ Outstanding fall color
○ Excellent summer foliage
○ Provides food and shelter for birds
○ Few bothersome pests and diseases
○ Loves wet, swampy sites
○ Grass will grow beneath the limbs

## Useful Hint

While the flowers are barely noticeable to humans, bees adore them, and tupelo honey (black gum is also known as black tupelo) is a popular southern favorite.

**Bloom Color**
White flowers but not showy

**Bloom Period**
Spring

**Height/Width**
50 feet x 30 feet

**Planting Location**
- Deep, well-drained acidic soil
- Full sun or a little shade

**Planting**
- Plant only in spring before new growth starts; black gum can be difficult to transplant.
- Dig the hole no deeper than the rootball and twice as wide.
- If tree is balled and burlapped, remove the burlap before placing the tree in the hole.
- Place the tree in the hole and fill in with soil dug from the hole.
- Water well.
- Make a saucer around the plant with any remaining soil.

**Watering**
- During the first year, water regularly, keeping the roots moist.
- When the tree is established, water thoroughly at least once a month during periods of drought.

*Easy Tip*

Choose plants in containers or smaller trees; black gum can be tricky to transplant due to its long tap-root.

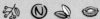

**Fertilizing**
- Each year, topdress using an acid-based mulch, or in spring, apply fertilizer formulated for acid-loving trees.

**Suggestions for Vigorous Growth**
- Do not prune or otherwise disrupt the main trunk or stem; this damages the tree's natural form.

**Pest Control**
- Few pests or diseases bother this tree.
- Yellowing leaves may be due to the soil's not being acidic enough—feed with acidic fertilizer.

**Complementary Plants**
- Black gum makes an excellent specimen tree for lawns.

**Recommended Selections**
- 'Jermyn's Flame' has larger leaves than the species.

# Blue Atlas Cedar

*Cedrus atlantica* 'Glauca'

## An Elegant Specimen Evergreen with Silvery-Blue Foliage

The only conifers (cone-bearing plants) that bloom in the fall, blue atlas cedars provide beautiful, dominant landscape features. They have angular, spurred branches adorned with tufts of stiff, bluish, 1- to 2-inch-long needles and decorative 3-inch cones. Younger trees have an open, irregular, erect, pyramidal shape. Mature ones become more flat topped with distinctly tiered horizontal branches, suggesting years of resistance to wind and weather challenges.

## Top Reasons to Plant

○ Unusual silvery-blue color
○ Attractive cones
○ Excellent specimen tree
○ Grows quickly when young
○ Pest and disease resistant
○ Distinctive mature shape
○ Drought tolerant when established

## Useful Hint

Fast-growing in youth, blue atlas cedars slow as they age and may live three hundred years or more, so be careful where you plant them!

**Bloom Color**
Blue-green evergreen foliage

**Bloom Period**
Foliage effective year-round

**Height/Width**
40 to 60 feet x 40 to 60 feet

**Planting Location**
- Prefers well-drained soil rich in organic matter but readily adapts to many soils
- Full sun or very light shade
- Requires a site protected from strong winds

**Planting**
- Plant in spring or fall.
- Dig a saucer-shaped hole just as deep as and at least twice as wide as the rootball.
- Set the rootball level with or slightly higher than the surrounding ground.
- Place the tree in the hole and fill in with soil dug from the hole.
- Form a saucer around the tree, using any remaining soil.
- Water well.

**Watering**
- Water young trees regularly until established.

**Fertilizing**
- Feed every year for the first four or five years.

## Easy Tip

Plant a blue atlas cedar near your house to accent a nice architectural feature.

**Suggestions for Vigorous Growth**
- Spread 2 to 3 inches of organic mulch over roots, not touching the trunk.
- Prune only to remove broken, rubbing, or awkward branches.
- Leave dropped needles under tree to act as mulch.

**Pest Control**
- Rodents sometimes nest in winter mulch and gnaw tender trunk bark.
- If rodents appear, wait until the ground freezes hard before spreading winter mulch.
- *Or* wrap vulnerable young cedar stems with hardware cloth.

**Complementary Plants**
- Best grown as an individual specimen.

**Recommended Selections**
- 'Argentea' has silvery-blue needles.
- 'Aurea' has yellowish needles and a narrow, stiff form.
- 'Glauca Pendula' has weeping branches and can be espaliered.

# Canadian Hemlock

*Tsuga canadensis*

## A Graceful, Stately Evergreen That Will Take Tennessee Heat

When I visit areas with cold climates, I admire the needled evergreens. Not just for their strong presence and deep color, but because I regret that we can grow so few of them in Tennessee. Sure, they're plenty winter-hardy, but they can't take the heat and humidity of a typical lowland Tennessee summer. An exception—despite the Canadian part of its name—is this stately tree. Its outer branches weep slightly, giving the tree a graceful appearance.

## Top Reasons to Plant

- Tolerates heat and humidity
- Thrives in shade or partial sun
- Graceful form
- Green all year
- Grows quickly
- Good hedge or screen

## Useful Hint

Canadian hemlock is right at home in shady yards and gardens.

## Bloom Color
Prized for its deep-green, soft-textured foliage

## Bloom Period
Foliage effective year-round

## Height/Width
40 to 90 feet x 25 to 35 feet

## Planting Location
• Moist but well-drained soil preferably containing lots of organic matter
• Tolerates sun with frequent watering; partial shade is ideal, but full shade is okay

## Planting
• Plant in early fall or spring.
• Dig the hole as deep as the rootball and twice as wide.
• Place the tree in the hole and fill in with soil dug from the hole.
• Water well.
• Mulch well.

## Watering
• Water regularly to keep soil moist especially when the tree is getting established and during dry spells.

## Fertilizing
• Fast grower, rarely needs fertilizer

## *Easy Tip*
Use Canadian hemlock as a fast-growing hedge or screen.

## Suggestions for Vigorous Growth
• If using as hedge or screen, shear in spring or summer for formal look, or thin branches for informal appearance

## Pest Control
• Large numbers of pests are potential problems, but most have little effect on well-maintained trees.

## Complementary Plants
• Grows nicely with shade-loving shrubs, such as evergreen azaleas, rhododendrons, mountain laurel, and oakleaf hydrangea.
• Does well with ferns, hostas, cardinal flower, and astilbe.

## Recommended Selections
• 'Golden Splendor' is a yellow-needled cultivar.
• 'Sargentii' is a beautiful weeping form that grows no taller than 15 feet but may be twice as wide.

# Carolina Silverbell

*Halesia tetraptera*

## A Charming Native with Clusters of Spring Blooms

Tennesseans have a fondness for spring-flowering trees, as witnessed by practically every neighborhood's being filled with dogwoods and redbuds. Carolina silverbell fits right into this trend. Its graceful white or pink bell-shaped blooms hang in delicate clusters along the branches in mid- to late spring before the leaves appear, and the fruits last into winter. I suggest growing it alone with your flowering dogwoods—they complement each other nicely.

## Top Reasons to Plant

- Beautiful spring flowers
- Fruits that last into winter
- Insect and disease resistant
- Requires little care
- Good alternative to flowering dogwood

## Useful Hint

Try to situate Carolina silverbell on a hill or slope so the flowers can be viewed from below.

**Bloom Color**
White or pink

**Bloom Period**
Spring

**Height/Width**
30 to 50 feet x 20 to 35 feet

**Planting Location**
• Moist, acidic soil that drains well and contains lots of organic matter
• Partial shade works best, but the plant will tolerate more sun

**Planting**
• Choose container-grown plants rather than balled-and-burlapped ones.
• Plant in early fall or in spring.
• Dig the hole as deep as the rootball and twice as wide.
• Place the tree in the hole and fill in with soil dug from the hole.
• Water well.
• Mulch well.

**Watering**
• Water often enough to keep soil moist—do not let it dry out.

**Fertilizing**
• Fertilizer is probably not needed.
• If the tree is not growing well, spread a high-nitrogen fertilizer for trees in a wide circle around the trunk after leaves fall in autumn.

*Easy Tip*

Experts recommend planting Carolina silverbell where dogwoods can't grow because of anthracnose. I concur.

**Suggestions for Vigorous Growth**
• Renew mulch as needed.
• Begin training the tree to a single trunk when it's young—otherwise, it becomes a large shrub, which isn't as attractive.
• Prune—never removing more than one-fourth of the growth in one year—in spring, after flowering.

**Pest Control**
• This tree resists insects and diseases well.

**Complementary Plants**
• Use as a nice understory tree with pines.
• Combine with lily-of-the-valley, evergreen azalea, rhododendrons, and with other spring-flowering trees for an attractive display.

**Recommended Selections**
• 'Rosea' has pink flowers.
• 'Arnold Pink' has larger flowers than those on the species.

# Chaste Tree

*Vitex agnus-castus*

## A Showy Small Tree with Spectacular Blue Blossoms

You may know chaste tree as a large shrub. Actually, it can be grown as a small tree or very large shrub, but I prefer it as a tree. Whichever way you want to train it, it belongs in your yard because of its spectacular 6- to 18-inch fragrant, blue flower spikes that appear at the end of summer and into fall. While not always winter-hardy in the coldest parts of Tennessee, chaste tree thrives in our hot summers.

## Top Reasons to Plant

- Beautiful blue blossoms late in the season
- Fragrant flowers
- Airy form
- Can be trained as shrub or small tree
- Compact size
- Tolerates heat and humidity
- Insect and disease resistant

## Bloom Color
Blue, lavender, white, or pink

## Bloom Period
Late summer to early fall

## Height/Width
8 to 25 feet x 15 to 20 feet

## Planting Location
- Prefers well-drained soil
- Full sun

## Planting
- If your're not planning to prune into a tree shape, place 20 feet from other plants.
- Plant in early spring.
- Dig the hole as deep as the rootball and twice as wide.
- Place the plant in the hole and water with transplanting solution to stimulate root growth.
- Fill in around roots with soil from the hole.
- Water well.
- Mulch well.

## Watering
- During the first two years, water whenever rainfall is less than an inch each week.
- When established, this plant can tolerate dry conditions, but it grows best with regular water.

## Easy Tip

Chaste tree's small size, interesting foliage, and late-season bloom make it an excellent patio tree.

## Fertilizing
- Fertilizer is not usually needed.
- If the plant is not growing well, feed with 1 pound of 10-10-10 fertilizer at the end of March or April.

## Suggestions for Vigorous Growth
- Remove lower limbs in very early spring to train to a tree shape.
- Prune to remove winter damage at same time.

## Pest Control
- In very rainy weather, leaf spots may appear but usually aren't serious.
- Few other insect or disease problems bother this tree.

## Complementary Plants
- Chaste tree is often included as part of a shrub border.

## Recommended Selections
- A slow grower, 'Blushing Spires' has pink flower panicles.
- Vigorous 'Silver Spire' features white blossoms.
- *Vitex negundo* may be a more reliable choice for colder areas of the state.

## Useful Hint

With the lower limbs trimmed off, chaste tree turns from a large shrub into an airy shade tree.

# Chinese Pistachio

*Pistacia chinensis*

## A Versatile Small Tree with Outstanding Fall Color

An excellent small- to medium-sized tree, Chinese pistachio tolerates a wide range of locations and soil conditions. Once established, it is deep rooted and drought tolerant. It also offers reliable fall color even in the mildest areas of the state, with beautiful yellow, red-orange, and red leaves. Its wood is very strong, so wind and ice do little damage.

## Top Reasons to Plant

○ Adapts to a wide range of soils
○ Beautiful fall foliage
○ Drought tolerant when established
○ Grass can grow beneath it
○ Pest and disease resistant
○ Grows quickly

## Useful Hint

Chinese pistachio tolerates hot, confined areas.

## Bloom Color
Non-showy spring bloom

## Bloom Period
Fall foliage in yellow, red-orange, and red; thick heads of small, reddish brown fruit or seeds in fall

## Height/Width
20 to 40 feet x 20 to 30 feet

## Planting Location
- Prefers moist, well-drained soil but tolerates a wide range of conditions
- Sun

## Planting
- Plant container-grown tree in fall or in early spring.
- Dig the hole as deep as the rootball and twice as wide.
- Place the tree in the hole and water with transplant solution.
- Fill with soil dug from the hole.
- Mulch well.

## Watering
- Water regularly until established.
- This tree tolerates drought once established but grows faster with regular watering.

## *Easy Tip*
Chinese pistachio grows quickly when fertilized and watered regularly.

## Fertilizing
- No fertilizer is required, but the tree grows more quickly with yearly fertilizer.

## Suggestions for Vigorous Growth
- Prune as needed when the tree is young to train its growth.

## Pest Control
- No serious pests or diseases trouble this tree.

## Complementary Plants
- Use in an informal naturalized grouping or as a specimen tree.

## Recommended Selections
- There are no known cultivars, so plant the species.

# Cornelian Cherry

*Cornus mas*

## An Excellent Small Tree Blooming in Very Early Spring

Every spring as we wait for the first flowers and other signs winter is ending, this surprisingly early blooming dogwood bursts into flower on leafless branches. Its bright-yellow flowers cover the tree *en masse*. In summer, the foliage is a lustrous green, and by August, red cherrylike fruits appear. In full sun, the fall color is reddish purple, and in winter, the flaky bark is interesting.

## Top Reasons to Plant

○ Offers interest in three seasons
○ Beautiful yellow blooms in very early spring
○ Bright-red fruits and purple leaves in fall
○ Attracts birds

## Useful Hint

The fruits of cornelian cherry can be made into jam, but if you don't eat them, the birds certainly will.

**Bloom Color**
Yellow

**Bloom Period**
Early spring

**Height/Width**
20 to 25 feet x 15 to 20 feet

**Planting Location**
- Adapts to most soil types except very wet or very dry
- Prefers sun for best growth and flowers but tolerates light shade

**Planting**
- Plant in spring—fall planting is less successful.
- Dig the hole as deep as the rootball and twice as wide.
- Place the plant in the hole and fill in with soil dug from the hole.
- Water well.
- Mulch well.

**Watering**
- Keep roots moist until established.

**Fertilizing**
- No fertilizer is required.

**Suggestions for Vigorous Growth**
- Nursery plants are available as single-stem trees or multistem shrubs.
- Prune only to remove dead, diseased, or dying branches.

*Easy Tip*

Cut branches of cornelian cherry in winter, put them in a vase on a warm windowsill, and you'll have fresh blooms for the house.

- On older specimens, prune to remove crowded growth.
- Bloom is showiest and growth most vigorous in colder parts of Tennessee.

**Pest Control**
- No serious insects or diseases bother this plant.

**Complementary Plants**
- Cornelian cherry is stunning massed against a backdrop of dark-needled evergreens.

**Recommended Selections**
- 'Golden Glory' features an upright form with heavy flowering.
- 'Variegata' has leaves mottled with creamy white markings.

# Dawn Redwood

*Metasequoia glyptostroboides*

## An Ancient Fast-Growing Conifer for a Larger Landscape

Dawn redwood was found growing wild in China in 1941, but the fossil record shows this tree is millions of years old. When you look at a dawn redwood, imagine pterodactyls flying above and a brontosaurus munching on nearby giant ferns. It makes an excellent fast-growing shade tree for a larger landscape. Its leaves are soft needles ½-inch long, and they fall from the tree each autumn after turning to russet.

## Top Reasons to Plant

○ Fast-growing
○ Symmetrical cone shape without pruning
○ Good shade tree
○ Loses needles in winter, allowing sun through
○ No serious pests or diseases
○ Interesting history—dates back to the dinosaurs

## Bloom Color
Prized for its soft green needles in summer, turning orange-brown in fall

## Bloom Period
Foliage effective spring through fall

## Height/Width
70 to 100 feet x 25 feet

## Planting Location
- Slightly acidic, well-drained soil that holds moisture
- Sun

## Planting
- Plant balled-and-burlapped tree in midautumn or early spring.
- Dig the hole as deep as the rootball and three to five times as wide.
- Place the tree in the hole and cut away all burlap, twine, or wire.
- Fill in with soil dug from the hole.
- Water well.
- Mulch with 2 inches of pine straw or wood chips.

## Watering
- Water regularly until established.
- If summer temperatures rise above 95 degrees Fahrenheit, water heavily each week.

## *Easy Tip*
Dawn redwood can grow 4 feet per year under good conditions.

## Fertilizing
- When tree is young, measure the thickness of the trunk 4 feet from ground, and in March and April, apply $1/2$ cup of 10-10-10 fertilizer for each inch of trunk thickness.
- Once the tree matures, little fertilizer is needed.

## Suggestions for Vigorous Growth
- Light pruning can be done anytime.
- If the young tree needs support, a stake placed 18 inches away from both sides of the trunk will keep it upright, but stake the tree so it can sway slightly.

## Pest Control
- No serious pests or diseases bother this tree.

## Complementary Plants
- Use as a specimen tree in a very large open area.

## Recommended Selections
- There are no cultivars, so plant the species.

## *Useful Hint*
Dawn redwood commands a lot of space, so don't plant it unless you can give it the room it needs.

# Deodar Cedar
*Cedrus deodara*

## A Graceful Evergreen That Makes a Strong Statement

Deodar cedar is a marvelous tree for the landscape on larger properties where evergreens are not cramped for space. Mature specimens look like distant mountains on the horizon. These trees mature at 70 feet, and their wide-spreading pyramidal form makes a statement wherever you plant them. But don't crowd them into small yards— neither they nor you will be happy with the results.

## Top Reasons to Plant

○ Beautiful, graceful evergreen
○ Wide-spreading, pyramidal form
○ Excellent for large, open areas
○ Fine texture and soft look
○ Drought tolerant when established
○ Tolerates heat and humidity
○ Grows relatively quickly

## Useful Hint

Deodar cedars aren't reliably hardy when the temperature drops below 0 degrees Fahrenheit. Most specimens in Knoxville were killed in a cold snap in the 1980s, so be careful where you plant them.

## Bloom Color
Prized for its dark-green, evergreen foliage

## Bloom Period
Foliage effective year-round

## Height/Width
70 feet x 40 feet

## Planting Location
• Well-drained, somewhat dry soil
• Sun or half shade

## Planting
• Plant container-grown trees from spring through early fall.
• Dig the hole as deep as the rootball and twice as wide.
• Place the tree in the hole and fill with soil dug from the hole.
• Water thoroughly.
• Mulch well.

## Watering
• If there's no rain, water three times the first week, twice the second week, then once every seven to ten days until strong new growth begins.
• Once established, this tree tolerates dry soils.

## Fertilizing
• In spring of the second growing season, apply a fertilizer high in nitrogen.
• Every two or three years thereafter, fertilize in spring.

## *Easy Tip*
Deodar cedar's fine texture and needlelike leaves make a pleasing backdrop for broadleaf shrub borders.

## Suggestions for Vigorous Growth
• Do not prune or stake unless there's good reason to do so.
• As the tree matures, some lower limbs die, which is natural.
• Do not try to grow grass within the drip line of the tree—leave it mulched.

## Pest Control
• No serious insects or diseases bother this tree.

## Complementary Plants
• Due to its stature, use deodar cedar as a specimen tree.

## Recommended Selections
• 'Shalimar' is the most cold hardy.

# Flowering Crabapple

*Malus* species and cultivars

## A Very Showy Spring Bloomer— but Handle with Care

Flowering crabapples are seductive trees, with their showy spring blossoms followed by small red, orange, or yellow fruits beloved by birds and which sometimes hang onto the tree until after the leaves drop. But be warned—crabapples are very disease prone, so purchase only named cultivars that are known to do well in your area. Otherwise, you'll either spend lots of time spraying or being unhappy with your sickly tree—or maybe even both. But the right crabapple will create a beautiful focal point in your yard.

## Top Reasons to Plant

○ Beautiful spring flowers
○ Handsome fruit
○ Nice winter silhouette
○ Compact scale good for small areas and one-story houses
○ The right cultivar requires little care

## Useful Hint

If you have an outside eating area and enjoy birds, plant a flowering crabapple where you can see it from the window; you'll enjoy the blooms, fruits, and foliage—as well as the visiting birds.

**Bloom Color**
White, pink, red, or blends

**Bloom Period**
Spring

**Height/Width**
10 to 25 feet x 15 to 30 feet

**Planting Location**
• Prefers deep, fertile, moist soils but tolerates most soil types
• Sun

**Planting**
• Plant in fall or early spring.
• Dig the hole twice as wide as and the same depth as the rootball.
• Place the tree in the hole and water with a transplanting solution.
• Fill the hole with soil dug from the hole.
• Water well and mulch with 3 inches of shredded bark, fine bark, or pine straw.

**Watering**
• Water regularly until established.
• Water deeply during drought periods.

**Fertilizing**
• For the first few years, fertilize in late fall with a high-nitrogen fertilizer for trees; apply according to label directions.

**Suggestions for Vigorous Growth**
• Prune in spring to maintain rounded form and to remove pencil-sized "water sprouts."
• Do not prune heavily after early June, or you'll remove next year's flowers.

**Pest Control**
• Few insect problems trouble this tree.

*Easy Tip*

Plant only named cultivars of crabapples that have proven disease-resistant in your part of the state.

• Disease problems—unless you have a disease-resistant cultivar—include fireblight, powdery mildew, apple scab, and cedar-apple rust.

**Complementary Plants**
• Plant in beds with annuals or perennials.

**Recommended Selections**
• For Middle Tennessee, Cheekwood Botanical Garden suggests 'Donald Wyman', which has pink to red buds opening to single white flowers, followed by bright-red, long-lasting fruit.
• For East Tennessee, Chattanooga's Urban Forestry Department recommends 'Prairiefire', with red buds opening to single, deep-pink blooms, and dark-red, long-lasting fruit; and 'Centurion', with red buds, single red flowers, and deep-red, long-lasting fruit.
• For West Tennessee, the Memphis Botanic Garden suggests 'Callaway', with pink buds, single white flowers, and large deep-red long-lasting fruit; and *Malus floribunda* (often called Japanese flowering crabapple), with deep-pink buds, lots of fragrant white blossoms, and small, yellow and red fruits.

# Flowering Dogwood
*Cornus florida*

## The Ultimate Spring-Flowering Tree for Tennessee

Is there any tree that says spring more eloquently than flowering dogwood? Clouds of white define our Tennessee landscapes in April, and the tree's brilliant-red leaves and berries enliven autumn. In mountain areas, an anthracnose disease has killed most of our flowering dogwoods, causing us to turn to kousa dogwoods. If this disease isn't a problem in your area, be sure to add a flowering dogwood to your landscape.

## Top Reasons to Plant

○ Beautiful clouds of spring flowers
○ Bright-red fall color
○ Late summer red berries that attract birds
○ Interesting bark
○ Attractive layered habit
○ Says "spring" like no other tree

## Useful Hint

Underplant your dogwood with low-growing spring-flowering shrubs—they not only look pretty, but discourage damage to the dogwood from mowers and string trimmers.

**Bloom Color**
White, pink, or red

**Bloom Period**
Spring

**Height/Width**
20 to 30 feet x 20 to 25 feet

**Planting Location**
- Moist, acidic, well-drained soil with lots of organic matter
- Avoid poorly drained soil.
- Prefers partial shade but can take quite a bit of sun

**Planting**
- Plant in spring.
- Dig the hole twice as wide as and the same depth as the rootball.
- Place the tree in the hole and fill with soil dug from the hole.
- Water thoroughly.
- Mulch well with pine straw.

**Watering**
- Do not let the soil dry out.
- Water when rainfall is less than normal, especially in hot weather.
- The more sun your dogwood gets, the more water it needs.

**Fertilizing**
- Fertilizer is probably not necessary.
- To encourage growth in young trees, spread a granular, high-nitrogen fertilizer for trees around the tree in fall; follow label directions.

*Easy Tip*

If anthracnose is killing or damaging dogwoods in your area, consider a kousa dogwood instead (see separate entry).

**Suggestions for Vigorous Growth**
- Maintain mulch year-round.
- Prune after flowering—if pruning is necessary.
- Leave lower limbs on trees to protect the trunk from cold and damage.

**Pest Control**
- This tree is susceptible to many diseases and insects.
- Most serious insects are borers, which often enter holes in trunks caused by lawn mowers or string trimmers.
- Flowering dogwood is subject to leaf spots during wet weather, but they are usually not damaging.
- Mildew can occur; it looks like white powder on the foliage.

**Complementary Plants**
- Underplant with evergreen azaleas and spring bulbs, such as tulips and daffodils.

**Recommended Selections**
- 'Cherokee Princess' has large flowers, blooms early, and seems to resist many fungal diseases.
- 'Big Apple' features extra-large berries and flowers.

# Fringe Tree
*Chionanthus virginicus*

## A Beautiful Flowering Tree That Extends the Spring Season

Many wonderful small trees flower in midspring. But why should the beautiful blooms depart your yard at the end of April? Fringe tree, which produces large, lacy clusters of white, fringelike flowers in May and June, is an excellent choice for extending the season. Also known as grancy graybeard, fringe tree may be grown as a large shrub, but I think it's more useful and looks better as a small tree.

## Top Reasons to Plant

- Showy blooms in late spring to early summer
- Berries in late summer that attract birds
- Compact size
- Adapts to a variety of soils
- Tolerates pollution and other urban conditions
- Fragrant flowers

**Bloom Color**
White blooms followed by bluish berries

**Bloom Period**
Late spring to early summer

**Height/Width**
12 to 30 feet x 10 to 25 feet

**Planting Location**
- Best in moist, well-drained, acidic soil containing some organic matter
- Prefers full sun

**Planting**
- Plant in early fall or early spring.
- Dig the hole twice as wide as and as deep as the rootball.
- Place the tree in the hole.
- Water well with transplanting solution.
- Fill with dirt dug from the hole.
- Mulch.

**Watering**
- Water when rainfall is less than an inch per week.

**Fertilizing**
- Spread compost or rotted leaves around the base of the tree each fall to feed it lightly.

## Easy Tip

Since fringe tree adapts well to urban life, it's good next to a patio or sidewalk—it's also beautiful near a water garden.

**Suggestions for Vigorous Growth**
- Fringe tree leafs out late—don't worry if it doesn't have leaves yet when other trees do.
- To maintain tree shape, train to one main trunk.
- Prune immediately after flowering if pruning is needed.

**Pest Control**
- Borers may be a problem, so keep lawn equipment from nicking holes in the trunk; such holes are entry points for borers.
- Scale—little brown "dots" on stems and beneath leaves—may appear but usually aren't a big problem.

**Complementary Plants**
- Fringe tree goes well with late-spring and early-summer shrubs.

**Recommended Selections**
- Chinese fringe tree (*Chionanthus retusus*) has smaller flowers than fringe tree, but flowers several weeks earlier.

## Useful Hint

Fringe tree produces bluish berries in August, which are much appreciated by a variety of birds.

# Ginkgo

*Ginkgo biloba*

## An Ancient Tree with Fan-Shaped Leaves Turning Clear-Yellow in Autumn

All it takes is one look, and you're hooked. One glance at the unusual fan-shaped leaves or the clear-yellow foliage that covers the whole tree in fall, and you'll want a ginkgo. When young, it has a gangly appearance, like an adolescent who's all arms and legs. But as the "ugly duckling" ages, it grows wider and more graceful, becoming one of the most rewarding shade trees available.

## Top Reasons to Plant

○ Beautiful, unusual leaf shape
○ Excellent yellow foliage in fall
○ Majestic, ancient appearance
○ Pest and disease resistant
○ Outstanding shade tree

## Useful Hint

Ginkgo is reportedly one hundred fifty million to two hundred million years old, and its intriguing appearance hints at its history.

## Bloom Color
Insignificant green blooms

## Bloom Period
Mid-spring

## Height/Width
25 to 50 feet x 15 to 40 feet

## Planting Location
- Loose, well-drained soil, alkaline or acidic
- Sun

## Planting
- Buy named cultivars—which will be male; female trees develop awful-smelling, messy fruits.
- Plant in fall or spring.
- Dig the hole twice as wide as and the same depth as the rootball.
- Place the tree in the hole and water with transplant solution.
- Fill with dirt dug from the hole.
- Mulch.

## Watering
- Water frequently after transplanting if weather is dry.
- Once established, water when rainfall is less than an inch per week.

## Fertilizing
- Fertilize in early years with 1 pound of 19-0-0 per inch of trunk diameter; apply in late fall after leaves are raked up.

## Suggestions for Vigorous Growth
- Young trees may need staking to stand upright.

### Easy Tip
Be sure to buy named cultivars of ginkgos to guarantee you have a male—the females produce nasty-smelling, messy fruit to be avoided at all costs.

- Do not attach stakes too tightly and remove them after one year.
- Prune in winter if needed.

## Pest Control
- No serious pests or diseases trouble this tree.

## Complementary Plants
- If you have room, plant a pair of ginkgos, preferably against a dark evergreen backdrop, where the yellow leaves will shine in fall.

## Recommended Selections
- 'Shangri-La'® turns an excellent golden-yellow in fall.
- The wider spreading 'Autumn Gold'™ also has outstanding fall color.

# Golden Rain Tree
*Koelreuteria paniculata*

## A Combination Shade and Flowering Tree with Gorgeous Yellow Blooms

Golden rain tree is unusual—it blooms in early spring, when few other trees do, and unlike most flowering trees, it's also a shade tree. In summer, golden rain tree develops clusters of copper-colored seedpods that hang on the tree decoratively until fall. But the real reason to grow this tree is its flowers—10- to 14-inch bright-yellow clusters. It's also nice that it tolerates just about any soil or climate conditions.

## Top Reasons to Plant

- Showy clusters of yellow flowers in summer
- Decorative seedpods until fall
- Tolerates many soils and climates
- Permits grass to grow under it
- Good shade tree in summer
- Grows quickly
- Drought tolerant when established

## Useful Hint

Because golden rain tree has such deep roots, it's easy to grow grass around it.

**Bloom Color**
Yellow

**Bloom Period**
Summer

**Height/Width**
30 to 40 feet x 25 to 35 feet

**Planting Location**
- Adapts to any well-drained soil, whether acidic or alkaline
- Sun
- A slightly protected site is welcome in the first few years.

**Planting**
- Plant container-grown or balled-and-burlapped trees in fall or spring.
- Dig the hole twice as wide as and as deep as the rootball.
- Place the tree in the hole, removing any synthetic burlap or twine.
- Water well with a transplanting solution.
- Fill with soil dug from the hole.
- Mulch lightly.

**Watering**
- Until established, water deeply when rainfall is less than an inch per week.
- After two years, the tree should tolerate drought.

**Fertilizing**
- This medium- to fast-growing tree rarely needs fertilizer.

## *Easy Tip*

Golden rain tree doesn't mind heat or wind, but the leaves on young trees may be nipped by late-spring frosts, so a slightly protected spot is welcome in the first years.

**Suggestions for Vigorous Growth**
- Golden rain tree rarely needs pruning—if it does, prune in winter.
- Remove damaged limbs any time.

**Pest Control**
- Few insects or diseases trouble this tree.

**Complementary Plants**
- Underplant with yellow annuals or perennials.
- For a beautiful look, plant blue hydrangeas near this tree.

**Recommended Selections**
- Bougainvillea golden rain tree (*Koelreuteria bipinnata*) is a smaller tree with yellow flowers in late summer and early autumn; it features more colorful seed capsules.

# Japanese Cryptomeria

*Cryptomeria japonica*

## A Fast-Growing Evergreen That Tolerates Tennessee Summers

The number of needled evergreens that tolerate our summer heat and humidity can be counted without running out of fingers. So if we want conical evergreens, sometimes we have to turn to trees whose names are hard to spell and pronounce. Call it Japanese cedar, if you prefer, but plant this fast-growing conifer, which officially has "leaves" instead of needles. The dwarf cultivars are especially interesting for small spaces.

## Top Reasons to Plant

- Tolerates summer heat and humidity
- Beautiful, graceful "needled" evergreen
- Adaptable to various soils and light conditions
- Excellent specimen tree
- Dwarf forms available for smaller properties
- Disease and insect resistant

## Useful Hint

Japanese cryptomeria makes an excellent hedge or screen.

## Bloom Color
Grown for its year-round foliage, dark-green in summer, sometimes purple or bronze in winter

## Bloom Period
Foliage effective year-round

## Height/Width
1 to 60 feet x 2 to 30 feet

## Planting Location
- Sheltered from strong winds
- Rich, moist, acidic, well-drained soil
- Sun or partial sun

## Planting
- Plant in early fall or early spring.
- Dig the hole twice as wide as and exactly as deep as the rootball.
- Place the tree in the hole and water with a transplanting solution.
- Fill with dirt that came from the hole.
- Mulch with organic matter.

## Watering
- This tree needs ample moisture to perform at its best.
- Water when weekly rainfall doesn't total an inch.

## Fertilizing
- Fertilizer is not usually needed, but granular high-nitrogen tree fertilizer may be spread at the base of the trunk in fall.
- Use 1 pound fertilizer for each inch of trunk diameter.

## *Easy Tip*
Look into the dwarf cultivars to plant in small spaces.

## Suggestions for Vigorous Growth
- This tree needs little pruning except to remove wayward growth.
- In early years, pinch the tips of stems in early summer to encourage denser growth.

## Pest Control
- Few insects and diseases trouble this tree.
- If the tips of stems or branches suffer dieback, consult the Extension Service for possible causes and cures.

## Complementary Plants
- Japanese cryptomeria makes a fine specimen tree where you want an evergreen presence in a prominent spot.
- This tree is ideal for Asian-type gardens.

## Recommended Selections
- The "needles" of many cultivars turn plum or bronze in winter, but those of 'Gyokuryu' tend to remain deep-green.
- 'Benjamin Franklin' also remains deep-green.

# Japanese Maple

*Acer palmatum*

## A Beautiful Tree with Many Forms that Tolerates Shade

Wow! That's a common reaction to a beautiful, mature Japanese maple. And it may also be the reaction to the price tag on a 2-foot plant at a nursery. But while the trees are often expensive, many gardeners believe they're well worth it. Their popularity is soaring with the increase in shade gardens. Due to a wide range of sizes, forms, leaves, and seasonal colors, there's a Japanese maple for every taste and place in the garden.

## Top Reasons to Plant

○ Stunning small trees
○ Beautiful spring, summer, and fall colors
○ Intriguing branch structure
○ Elegant choice for shady gardens
○ Excellent near water gardens
○ Insect and disease resistant

## Useful Hint

Japanese maples come in sizes from a small mound to a tall tree, forms from upright to cascading, with leaves that are lobed like a regular maple or finely dissected and lacy, and seasonal colors of yellow, red, purple, and green.

## Bloom Color
Insignificant purple blooms

## Bloom Period
Late spring

## Height/Width
6 to 40 feet x 8 to 30 feet

## Planting Location
- Moist, well-drained soil containing organic matter
- Partial shade—dappled shade beneath tall trees is ideal

## Planting
- Plant from spring until early fall.
- Dig the hole twice as wide as and as deep as the rootball.
- Water with transplanting solution.
- Fill with soil dug from the hole.
- Mulch well.

## Watering
- Never let this tree dry out.
- It is especially important to keep the soil moist when the plant is young and during droughts.

## Fertilizing
- Spread high-nitrogen fertilizer for trees in late fall.

## Suggestions for Vigorous Growth
- Maintain mulch year-round.
- Do not prune off lower limbs—they add grace and charm to the tree.

## Easy Tip
Seed-grown Japanese maples cost less than named cultivars, but you won't know their eventual size or form. If you want one whose leaves remain red in summer, buy one in summer.

## Pest Control
- Few pests bother this tree.

## Complementary Plants
- Japanese maple makes an elegant focal point for partially shaded yards.
- Cascading types add appeal near water gardens.

## Recommended Selections
- 'Bloodgood' is the most tolerant Japanese maple I've grown—it endures extreme heat and cold, sun and shade, and its leaves stay consistently red all year.
- 'Red Dragon', which has dissected leaves, also stays red all year.

# Japanese Stewartia

*Stewartia pseudocamellia*

## A Beautiful Small Tree with Lots of Assets

Stewartias bear camellia-like flowers in mid- to late summer when little else blooms. They not only have creamy-white flowers, but also have colorful fall foliage and peeling bark that shows cinnamon, red, gray, and shades of orange. Purple-bronze leaves emerge in early spring. In summer, the leaves turn green; in winter, they change to purple-orange, yellow, and bronze-red.

## Top Reasons to Plant

- Gorgeous, camellia-like blooms
- Beautiful fall color
- Interesting, colorful winter bark
- Pest and disease resistant
- Flowers in late summer
- Excellent small tree

## Useful Hint

It's not unusual for Japanese stewartia to take three to five years to become a fully established, full-blooming plant, but it's definitely worth the wait.

## Bloom Color
Creamy-white petals with orange anthers

## Bloom Period
Mid- to late summer

## Height/Width
30 to 40 feet x 20 to 30 feet

## Planting Location
- Fertile, moist, acidic soil containing lots of organic matter
- Sun is best for flowers and fall color; in warmer parts of the state, some shade at noon is appreciated

## Planting
- Plant small, young, container-grown or balled-and-burlapped trees in early spring while they are still dormant.
- Dig the hole three times as wide as and as deep as the rootball.
- Set the plant in the hole so the crown (where trunk and roots meet) is an inch above ground level.
- Fill with dirt dug from the hole.
- Shape the earth around the crown into wide saucer.
- Water slowly and deeply.
- Apply mulch 3 inches deep and 3 inches away from the trunk.

## Watering
- During the first year, in weeks without an inch of rain, water the tree deeply.

## Easy Tip
If you're spreading lime on the lawn, keep it at least 2 feet outside stewartia's drip line—this tree doesn't like lime.

## Fertilizing
- Apply slow-release, acidic fertilizer in late winter or early spring.
- Water fertilizer in well.

## Suggestions for Vigorous Growth
- Maintain mulch year-round.

## Pest Control
- No serious pests or diseases bother this tree.

## Complementary Plants
- Japanese stewartia makes a beautiful lawn specimen.
- Group in a shrub border with low-growing azaleas.

## Recommended Selections
- Korean stewartia (*Stewartia koreana*) may be a better fit for small gardens, growing to 20 to 30 feet, but is otherwise similar to Japanese stewartia.
- Chinese stewartia (*Stewartia sinensis*) is smaller still, reaching 15 to 25 feet, with otherwise similar attributes.

# Japanese Zelkova
*Zelkova serrata*

## A Fast-Growing Shade Tree Reminiscent of the Elm

We Americans are impatient. When we plant a tree, we want it to be big as soon as possible. So when we buy a tree, the first question we ask is, "How quickly does it grow?" That leads to many bad choices, because fast-growing trees usually develop problems. That's *not* true of Japanese zelkova, which may grow several feet a year when young. It's a well-mannered tree with foliage similar to the elm and with interesting bark.

## Top Reasons to Plant

- Fast growing but strong
- Interesting winter bark
- Excellent substitute for the elm
- Pollution resistant
- Few pests and diseases
- Good shade tree
- Drought tolerant when established

## Useful Hint

The bark on a Japanese zelkova is reddish when the tree is young, changing to gray and mottled on mature specimens.

**Bloom Color**
Insignificant blooms

**Bloom Period**
Spring

**Height/Width**
50 to 90 feet x 40 to 60 feet

**Planting Location**
- Moist, well-drained soil, either acidic or alkaline
- Sun

**Planting**
- Plant from spring through fall.
- Dig the hole twice as wide as and as deep as the rootball.
- Place the tree in the hole, removing any synthetic burlap or twine.
- Water well with transplanting solution.
- Using soil dug from the hole, pack the soil around the tree's roots.
- Mulch lightly with pine straw, shredded leaves, or fine pine bark.

**Watering**
- Water deeply but regularly in the early years.
- Once established, this tree's deep root system helps it tolerate drought.

**Fertilizing**
- This tree grows well without fertilizer.
- If a late frost kills young leaves, fertilize in late fall with high-nitrogen tree fertilizer spread in a circle around the tree's base according to package directions.
- Water fertilizer in well.

*Easy Tip*

This pollution-resistant tree is a good choice for urban areas or near highways.

**Suggestions for Vigorous Growth**
- Spring frosts may damage the leaves of young trees, but the leaves grow back.
- Prune in winter as needed, removing any crowded branches.

**Pest Control**
- This tree occasionally suffers from disease or insects, especially beetles, but the problem is usually not serious.

**Complementary Plants**
- Japanese zelkova makes an ideal shade tree.

**Recommended Selections**
- 'Green Vase'® grows especially quickly and has more consistent fall color than many zelkovas.

# Katsura Tree

*Cercidiphyllum japonicum*

## A Beautiful, Refined Shade Tree Planted for Its Foliage

Katsura is a beautiful, fast- to medium-fast-growing, refined shade tree with outstanding foliage. The new leaves in spring are a bronze or reddish purple, changing to blue-green in summer, then in fall transformed to a spectacular, glowing, apricot-orange and golden yellow—a sight worth traveling to see. The aging leaves give off a faint, spicy scent. The tree has a dense rounded form and shaggy brown bark that add interest to the winter landscape.

## Top Reasons to Plant

- Beautiful leaves shaped like those of a redbud
- Fast growing
- Spectacular fall foliage
- Shaggy brown bark interesting in winter
- Fragrant leaves
- Few pests and diseases
- Outstanding shade tree for medium-sized landscapes

## Useful Hint

The noted plantsman and author Michael Dirr says, "If I could use only one tree, this would be my first tree."

54

## Bloom Color

Grown for its leaves, which emerge bronze or reddish purple, change to bluish green in summer, then turn apricot-orange and gold in fall

## Bloom Period

Foliage effective spring through fall

## Height/Width

40 to 50 feet x 20 to 30 feet

## Planting Location

- Well-drained, moist, acidic soil with lots of organic matter
- Sun

## Planting

- Choose a *young*, dormant, container-grown or balled-and-burlapped tree—this tree does not easily transplant successfully.
- Plant in early spring.
- Dig the hole three times the width of the rootball and as deep.
- Set the tree in the hole so the crown (where trunk and roots meet) is an inch or so above ground level.
- Fill in with soil dug from the hole.
- With remaining soil, make a wide saucer around the tree.
- Water slowly and deeply.
- Apply 3 inches of mulch starting 3 inches from the trunk.

## Watering

- In the first year, unless a soaking rain falls, water the tree thoroughly every week.

## *Easy Tip*

Be sure to buy a single-stemmed plant to ensure a strong, straight trunk.

- For the first two or three years, water deeply as often as you water flowers.

## Fertilizing

- Apply high-nitrogen fertilizer in late winter.
- Water fertilizer in well.

## Suggestions for Vigorous Growth

- Maintain mulch year-round.
- Prune in late winter to feature the trunk and create a broad crown.

## Pest Control

- No serious pests or diseases trouble this tree.

## Complementary Plants

- Katsura is best used as a specimen tree where it can be seen year-round.

## Recommended Selections

- The species is highly recommended.
- The weeping form, 'Pendula', is a lovely small tree that grows to 15 to 25 feet tall.

# Kousa Dogwood
*Cornus kousa*

## An Excellent Substitute for the Native Flowering Dogwood

Gardeners do a double-take when they see a dogwood still in bloom in May or even June. It's the kousa dogwood, a tree that blooms weeks later than the native flowering dogwood. And the kousa dogwood comes into its glory after its leaves have emerged. The leaves are more slender than those of the flowering dogwood and appear to be a deeper green. In fall, seeds appear in tight clusters, resembling a red raspberry rising above the branch tip.

## Top Reasons to Plant

- Beautiful white flowers in late spring through early summer
- Showy red fruits in late summer
- Reddish purple or scarlet leaves in fall
- Resists anthracnose disease, which affects native dogwoods
- Tolerates more sun than flowering dogwoods
- Horizontal branching habit attractive in winter
- Interesting bark in winter

## Bloom Color
White

## Bloom Period
Late spring through early summer

## Height/Width
10 to 20 feet x 10 to 20 feet

## Planting Location
- Well-drained, acidic soil with lots of organic matter
- Sun but with afternoon shade

## Planting
- Plant in spring.
- Dig the hole three times as wide as and the same depth as the rootball.
- Place the tree in the hole and cut away any burlap, wire, and twine.
- Fill with soil dug from the hole.
- Water thoroughly.
- Spread a 2-inch layer of pine straw or wood chips over the planting area, starting 2 inches away from the trunk.

## Watering
- Water well until established.
- If summer temperatures go above 95 degrees Fahrenheit and there's little rain, water heavily each week even if the tree is established.

## *Easy Tip*
Keep a wide band of mulch around the trunk so mowers and string trimmers can't come close enough to create wounds through which diseases and insects can enter.

## Fertilizing
- In early spring or late fall apply 1 cup of 10-10-10 fertilizer for each inch of thickness of trunk 4 feet above ground.

## Suggestions for Vigorous Growth
- Light pruning may be done anytime if needed.
- Keep mulch in place year-round.

## Pest Control
- Kousa dogwood resists borers and anthracnose disease.

## Complementary Plants
- Plant with spring- and early-summer-flowering shrubs and perennials.

## Recommended Selections
- The flowers of 'Moonbeam' may reach 8 inches wide.
- *Cornus kousa* var. *chinensis* 'Milky Way', a form of kousa dogwood, has numerous flowers and a bushy form nice for smaller landscapes.

## *Useful Hint*
Kousa dogwood resists the anthracnose disease that has killed so many flowering dogwoods in the South and East, and it seems to resist dogwood borer, as well.

# Kwanzan Cherry

*Prunus serrulata* 'Kwanzan'

## A Beautiful Spring-Flowering Cherry with Double Pink Blooms

Thanks to cherry blossom festivals, flowering cherries are gaining attention and becoming an increasing presence in the spring landscape. The Kwanzan cherry is one of the best, known for large, double, rosy-pink flowers and leaves that are reddish when new and bronze in fall. It offers a spectacular blooming display in spring, as it is a very free-flowering tree.

## Top Reasons to Plant

- Beautiful spring show of blooms
- Attractive bark
- Relatively small stature
- Good cut flower
- Fragrant blooms
- Nice fall color

## Useful Hint

It seems inelegant to say anything negative about such a beautiful show, but fallen blooms should be cleaned immediately from the deck or patio—they're quite slippery.

## Bloom Color
Deep pink

## Bloom Period
Spring

## Height/Width
15 to 20 feet x 15 to 25 feet

## Planting Location
- Fast-draining soil that contains organic matter
- Full sun

## Planting
- Plant in spring or early autumn.
- In clay soils, consider planting Kwanzan cherry on a mound or in a raised bed to avoid the possibility of root rot.
- Dig the hole as deep as the rootball and twice as wide.
- Place the tree in the hole and water with transplanting solution.
- Fill in around roots with soil from the hole.
- Water well.
- Mulch with 2 to 3 inches of organic matter.

## Watering
- Water when rainfall measures less than an inch per week.
- Be careful not to overwater in clay soil.

## Fertilizing
- If blooms have been sparse, fertilize in late fall with a high-nitrogen fertilizer for trees, following label directions.

# Easy Tip
Cut branches of flowering cherry while in bloom to use in arrangements.

## Suggestions for Vigorous Growth
- Prune as necessary after flowers fade.
- Maintain light mulch to prevent trunk damage from lawn equipment.

## Pest Control
- Insects and diseases are often troublesome—affected trees tend not to be long-lived.
- Bacterial canker and bot canker, appearing as oozing areas on the bark, may occur.
- Consult the Extension Service for causes and cures for any problems that arise.

## Complementary Plants
- Underplant with spring-flowering bulbs in companionable colors.

## Recommended Selections
- 'Amanogawa' is quite columnar, about 20 feet tall and only 5 feet wide.
- 'Royal Burgundy' has deep-pink flowers and a lovely mahogany-red trunk.

# Lacebark Elm
*Ulmus parvifolia*

## A Disease-Resistant Elm with Fabulous Bark

Few people pay much attention to a tree's bark. We look for colorful flowers and foliage instead. But once you've seen the shedding and mottled bark of the lacebark elm, you'll never think of bark as dull again. Eye-catching bark is especially important now that many of us want landscapes that have something of interest in all four seasons. Lacebark elm also resists Dutch elm disease and Japanese beetles, and it has good fall color.

## Top Reasons to Plant

○ Beautiful bark showy in winter
○ Disease and insect resistant
○ Good fall color
○ Adaptable to different soils
○ Tough and durable
○ Excellent shade tree

## Useful Hint

Don't confuse this tree, which is sometimes called Chinese elm, with Siberian elm (*Ulmus pumila*), a fast-growing tree that is *not* recommended.

**Bloom Color**
Inconsequential

**Bloom Period**
Late summer

**Height/Width**
40 to 50 feet x 30 to 50 feet

**Planting Location**
- Well-drained soil, either acidic or alkaline, but best results are in moist soil with organic matter
- Full sun

**Planting**
- Plant in fall or spring.
- Dig the hole as deep as the rootball and twice as wide.
- Place the tree in the hole and remove any synthetic twine or burlap.
- Water with transplanting solution.
- Fill with dirt dug from the hole.
- Mulch with 2 to 3 inches of organic matter.

**Watering**
- When the tree is young, water regularly when rainfall doesn't amount to an inch per week.

**Fertilizing**
- Fertilizer is usually not needed.
- Decomposing mulch gently feeds the tree.

*Easy Tip*

As this tree grows, remove its lower limbs to show off the gorgeous bark.

**Suggestions for Vigorous Growth**
- After the tree reaches moderate size, remove one or two of the lowest limbs each winter until the lowest limbs are at least 8 feet off the ground.

**Pest Control**
- This tree resists diseases and pests.

**Complementary Plants**
- Lacebark elm makes an excellent specimen tree where its bark can be seen and appreciated.

**Recommended Selections**
- 'Golden Rey' has yellow leaves all season—clear-yellow when they open and gold by fall.
- 'Dynasty' develops a nice rounded shape and features orange-yellow leaves in fall.

# Leyland Cypress

*Cupressaceae × cupressocyparis leylandii*

*A Tall, Fast-Growing Evergreen Excellent for Screening*

Leyland cypress has become almost a household word in many places, as there are few evergreens that grow so vigorously when planted as a privacy screen. It has an upright, columnar form similar to our native red cedars, but offers a softer, more pleasing appearance. It tolerates heavy shearing and makes a fine, tall hedge. Unpruned, it has graceful branches and bluish green feathery foliage.

## Top Reasons to Plant

○ Fast-growing evergreen
○ Useful for screening or tall hedge
○ Feathery, bluish green foliage
○ Attractive, scaly red-brown bark
○ Tolerates heavy shearing or pruning

## Useful Hint

Leyland cypress grows up to 3 feet per year, so it reaches 60 to 70 feet very quickly for an evergreen.

## Bloom Color
Grown for its soft, blue-green foliage

## Bloom Period
Foliage effective year-round

## Height/Width
40 to 50 feet x 40 to 50 feet

## Planting Location
- Well-drained, fertile soil with organic matter so it holds moisture
- Sun or some morning shade

## Planting
- Plant in early spring or late fall.
- Dig the hole three times as wide as and as deep as the rootball.
- If planting a hedge, make the planting bed 5 feet wide and space plants 3 to 5 feet apart.
- Place the tree in the hole and fill with a mixture of 2 parts soil and 1 part soil conditioner. Water thoroughly.
- Mulch 1 to 3 inches deep—but mulch should not touch the trunk.

## Watering
- Water regularly, especially the first year.

## Fertilizing
- A year after planting, feed with slow-release fertilizer.

## Suggestions for Vigorous Growth
- Too much water can lead to root rot.
- Stake plants 5 feet tall or shorter on the windward side.
- Prune moderately in late winter or in spring, if needed.
- Do not remove more than one-third of the foliage in any one season.

## Easy Tip
Nothing beats Leyland cypress for fast growth as an evergreen screen or hedge, but it requires pruning and a good bit of room, and is susceptible to several diseases—so consider carefully.

## Pest Control
- This tree is subject to cypress canker, which begins with the death of a lower branch.
- There's no chemical control for cypress canker, so remove affected limbs or entire trees.
- Bagworms may appear and can be life threatening to the tree.

## Complementary Plants
- Use as an evergreen backdrop for flowering trees and shrubs.
- Leyland cypress makes an excellent specimen evergreen.

## Recommended Selections
- 'Monca' and 'Irish Mint' are colorful and compact.
- 'Naylor's Blue', which grows 30 to 40 feet tall, has bright, gray-blue foliage intensely colored in winter.
- 'Castlewellan Gold'® is narrow, grows to 20 feet, and is tipped bronze-gold in winter.

# Norway Spruce

*Picea abies*

### A Classic Evergreen That Withstands Tennessee Summers

For Tennesseans who love and admire the classic, pyramidal, needled spruce trees that do so well for our northern cousins, the best choice is the Norway spruce. If you want a living Christmas tree, this is the one to buy. But be sure you have enough space to accommodate it after it leaves the living room—Norway spruces grow pretty quickly, and they ultimately reach at least 30 feet wide by 40 to 60 feet tall.

## Top Reasons to Plant

- Graceful, beautiful evergreen
- Tolerates heat and humidity
- Grows quickly
- Excellent tall screen or windbreak
- Withstands dry soil when established

## Useful Hint

If you have adequate room to show it off, the Norway spruce makes a majestic specimen plant—a row of them is also useful as a large-scale screen or windbreak.

## Bloom Color
Grown for its dark evergreen needles

## Bloom Period
Foliage effective year-round

## Height/Width
40 to 60 feet x 25 to 30 feet

## Planting Location
- Prefers moist, slightly acidic, well-drained soil
- Sun

## Planting
- Plant balled-and-burlapped or container-grown trees anytime of the year when the soil is workable.
- Dig the hole twice as wide as and as deep as the rootball.
- Set the tree in the hole and fill with dirt from the hole.
- Water thoroughly.
- Mulch with 2 to 3 inches of organic material.

## Watering
- Water well in early years to help the tree become established.
- Make sure the soil is well watered in the fall to help the tree live safely through the winter.

## Fertilizing
- Apply slow-release fertilizer for trees in the spring.

## Suggestions for Vigorous Growth
- Stake large specimens during the first growing season to reduce wind damage.

## Easy Tip
If planting Norway spruce as a screen or windbreak, space trees 18 to 20 feet apart.

## Pest Control
- *Cytospora* fungus may appear, causing the browning and death of branches, usually starting at the bottom of the plant—remove infected branches, and mulch to discourage grass and weed growth that limits air movement.
- Spruce gall aphid, causing a cone-shaped growth on the branches, may appear but generally isn't life threatening.

## Complementary Plants
- Norway spruce makes an excellent backdrop for shrubs with colorful bark, winter stems, or early spring flowers.
- Plant with 'Arnold Promise' witchhazel or the colorful twigs of the redtwig dogwood.

## Recommended Selections
- 'Cupressina', a narrow, upright cultivar, is good for planting in cities and confined landscapes.

# Ornamental Pear
*Pyrus calleryana*

### *A Showy Spring Bloomer with Better Choices Than 'Bradford'*

Most people refer to this tree as "Bradford pear." That's the name of the first and most commonly planted cultivar, but many other cultivars have the characteristic white flowers early in spring, glossy green leaves in summer, and excellent fall foliage color. *All* are better than 'Bradford', which has what experts call narrow crotch angles, which often cause limbs to break and the tree to split in half.

## Top Reasons to Plant

○ White flowers in early spring
○ Glossy green leaves in summer
○ Beautiful fall color
○ Good for screening
○ Tolerates dry soil when established
○ Few insect problems

## *Useful Hint*

Avoid planting the 'Bradford' cultivar, which has lots of structural problems—instead, choose another variety of ornamental pear.

## Bloom Color
White

## Bloom Period
Early spring

## Height/Width
30 to 50 feet x 16 to 35 feet

## Planting Location
- Tolerates many types of soil as long as it's well-drained
- Sun

## Planting
- Plant in late winter or early spring.
- Dig the hole as deep as the rootball and twice as wide.
- Place the tree in the hole and water with a transplanting solution.
- Pack soil from the hole around the rootball.
- Water thoroughly.
- Mulch lightly.

## Watering
- When the tree is young, water deeply when there's been less than an inch of rain in a week.

## Fertilizing
- No fertilizer is needed.

## Suggestions for Vigorous Growth
- Prune as needed in late winter.

## Easy Tip
Ornamental pears grow to be very large trees—space and site them according to their mature height and spread.

## Pest Control
- Insects are rarely a problem.
- Fireblight may occur, causing leaves and stems to appear as if boiling water had been poured over them—immediately prune back to nondiseased wood, disinfecting the saw or pruners between cuts.

## Complementary Plants
- This tree has a stiff, formal appearance that looks out of place in informal or naturalistic landscapes, so put it in a more formal, stylized setting.

## Recommended Selections
- 'Chanticleer'® is narrower than 'Bradford' and resists fireblight.
- 'Edgewood' has silvery-green foliage.
- 'Fauriei' has a pyramidal shape.
- Good for small yards, 'Korean Sun'® grows about 12 feet tall and 15 feet wide.

# Paperbark Maple

*Acer griseum*

### A Beautiful Four-Season Tree That Fits Most Yards

Imagine cinnamon-colored bark flaking naturally off a tree in thin sheets. Then place this intriguing bark on a 25-foot tree with a striking silhouette in winter, scarlet leaves in fall, and small flowers that develop into decorative winged seedpods. The result? Paperbark maple, a tree that keeps your interest in every season. It has a delicate texture in summer and is the right size to fit into almost every yard.

## Top Reasons to Plant

- Beautiful, reddish brown, peeling bark
- Outstanding fall foliage
- Suitable for small yards
- Interesting seedpods
- No serious pests or diseases
- Needs little maintenance
- Excellent near windows where its winter bark can be admired

## Useful Hint

This tree makes a good focal point for a small yard or along the sunny edge of the woods on a larger property.

## Bloom Color
Inconspicuous blooms

## Bloom Period
Spring

## Height/Width
25 to 30 feet x 12 to 30 feet

## Planting Location
- Prefers moist, well-drained soil but is adaptable
- Sun

## Planting
- Plant in spring.
- Dig the hole twice as wide as the rootball and as deep.
- Place the tree in the hole and water well with transplanting solution.
- Fill with soil dug from the hole.
- Mulch with pine straw or other organic matter.

## Watering
- Don't let the soil dry out.
- Water regularly if the soil isn't naturally moist and rainfall is lacking.

## Fertilizing
- This tree grows slowly (less than 1 foot per year) unless fertilized.
- For faster growth, feed in late fall with 1 pound of granular 19-0-0 fertilizer for each inch of trunk diameter or with a high-nitrogen tree fertilizer according to label directions.

## Easy Tip

*Easy Tip*

If you've been looking for something wonderfully different in a tree, paperbark maple is it.

- Spread fertilizer in a widening circle around the tree, beginning 6 inches from the trunk.

## Suggestions for Vigorous Growth
- This tree rarely needs pruning.
- If pruning is required, do it in winter.
- Maintain year-round mulch to keep moisture in the soil.
- Fertilize regularly for faster growth.

## Pest Control
- No serious pest problems trouble this tree.

## Complementary Plants
- Paperbark maple fits nicely into a shrub border.

## Recommended Selections
- Few cultivars are available yet, but 'Gingerbread'™ ('Ginzam') and 'Cinnamon Flake' are both excellent.

# Persian Ironwood

*Parrotia persica*

*A Choice Small Tree That's Attractive All Year*

This witchhazel relative is a beauty in every season. It has unusual blooms before it leafs out—closely packed red stamens are surrounded by a woolly brown bract, giving the overall tree a crimson glow. The leaves emerge reddish purple, then change to lustrous dark-green for summer, but the real show begins in fall. Persian ironwood's leaves first turn golden-yellow, then pinkish orange, and finally scarlet.

## Top Reasons to Plant

- Stunning fall foliage
- Small scale makes it suitable for most yards
- Beautiful scaling bark gives winter interest
- Pest and disease free
- Picturesque branching structure
- Drought resistant when established

## Useful Hint

Depending on the seed source, Persian ironwood can grow as a multistemmed large shrub or a more upright tree—some pruning is needed in its youth to give it the form you prefer.

## Bloom Color
Reddish brown

## Bloom Period
Late winter through early spring

## Height/Width
20 to 40 feet x 15 to 30 feet

## Planting Location
- Average, well-drained soil—it won't tolerate standing water
- Sun or light shade

## Planting
- Plant balled-and-burlapped trees in early spring.
- Dig the hole twice as wide as and as deep as the rootball.
- Place the tree in the hole and fill with soil from the hole.
- Water well.
- Mulch with 3 inches of shredded bark, fine bark, or pine straw.

## Watering
- The first couple of seasons, water deeply in weeks with less than an inch of rain.
- Though drought tolerant once established, this tree appreciates occasional watering during dry spells.

## *Easy Tip*

Persian ironwood is very dramatic in the winter garden once it reaches the age that its bark begins peeling.

## Fertilizing
- No fertilizer is needed.

## Suggestions for Vigorous Growth
- Prune in spring in the early years to create a graceful shape.

## Pest Control
- This tree is pest and disease free.

## Complementary Plants
- For a dramatic fall display, plant Persian ironwood with other members of the witchhazel family—witchhazel, fothergilla, and winter hazel.
- Underplant with hellebores and epimediums.

## Recommended Selections
- 'Pendula' is a weeping form.

# Pin Oak

*Quercus palustris*

## A Stately Shade Tree with a Distinctive Shape

Oaks are the trees we plant for posterity. They embody strength and majesty. We can grow many oaks in Tennessee, but certainly one of the best is the pin oak, which thrives even in wet soil. One of the curiosities of the pin oak is that its lower branches droop toward the ground and, even if you cut them off, the next higher layer of branches develops the drooping look.

## Top Reasons to Plant

○ Distinctive shape
○ Easily transplanted
○ Tolerates wet soils
○ Large, majestic shade tree
○ Adapts well to city conditions
○ Good fall color

## Useful Hint

Pin oak must have acidic soil—without it, this tree develops chlorosis (yellowish leaves).

## Bloom Color
Grown for its foliage

## Height/Width
60 to 70 feet x 25 to 40 feet

## Planting Location
- Prefers moist, rich, acidic, well-drained soil
- Tolerates wet soil
- Sun

## Planting
- Plant in late winter, when the tree is dormant.
- Dig the hole twice as wide and as deep as the rootball.
- Set the tree in the hole and remove any twine or burlap.
- Water with transplanting solution.
- Fill with soil from the hole.
- Mulch with 3 inches of shredded bark, fine bark, or pine straw.

## Watering
- Water deeply when the tree is young and rainfall doesn't total an inch per week.

## Fertilizing
- Feed the second through fourth years with a high-nitrogen tree fertilizer in late fall.

## *Easy Tip*
Many pin oaks hold their fall leaves until the next spring, sometimes late in spring, so don't worry if yours is late leafing out.

## Suggestions for Vigorous Growth
- One of the faster growing oaks (reaching 12 to 15 feet over five to seven years), it grows even more rapidly with regular watering and fertilizing.

## Pest Control
- Gypsy moths and galls may be a problem—consult the Extension Service for remedies.

## Complementary Plants
- Pin oak makes a good specimen tree in large settings.

## Recommended Selections
- 'Sovereign' has lower branches that do not weep.

# Purple Leaf Plum

*Prunus cerasifera*

## A Lovely Small Tree with Pink Blossoms and Purple Leaves

Purple leaf plum puts on a striking show all summer with its dark purple-red leaves, which may attract a good bit of attention from passersby. The tree blooms in early spring with small, showy white or pink blossoms covering it entirely. It's a relatively small tree that fits well into urban yards and gardens. If you're looking for spring to fall color for your yard, take a look at the purple leaf plum.

## Top Reasons to Plant

○ Beautiful spring blossoms
○ Richly colored leaves all summer and fall
○ Small scale fits into most settings
○ Adds good color near patios, decks, and gazebos
○ Can be used in large containers or planters

**Bloom Color**
White, pink, or purple

**Bloom Period**
Spring

**Height/Width**
15 to 25 feet x 10 to 20 feet

**Planting Location**
- Moist, well-drained, fertile soil
- Sun

**Planting**
- Plant container-grown or balled-and-burlapped trees in spring.
- Dig the hole twice as wide as and as deep as the rootball.
- Set the tree in the hole and water with a transplant solution.
- Fill with soil from the hole.
- Water well.
- Mulch with 3 to 4 inches of bark.

**Watering**
- Water as needed to prevent the soil from drying out.

**Fertilizing**
- Beginning a year after planting, feed with a long-lasting, slow-release fertilizer.

*Easy Tip*

Purple leaves make a real statement in the landscape, so make sure they mix comfortably with the other colors in your yard.

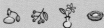

**Suggestions for Vigorous Growth**
- Prune to shape in early spring.
- Remove dead branches and twigs anytime.

**Pest Control**
- Fireblight may be a problem—consult the Extension Service for controls.
- Peach tree borers may attack unhealthy trees, so keep yours in good shape.

**Complementary Plants**
- Purple leaf plum looks nice as a focal point in an otherwise green setting.
- Use in a landscape with other red- or purple-leaved plants, such as loropetalum and the purple-leaved forms of barberry.

**Recommended Selections**
- 'Atropurpurea' is the most widely available, with ruby-red new leaves, turning wine-colored, then becoming dark reddish purple.
- 'Hollywood' has green leaves that turn deep-purple.
- 'Purpusii' has variegated leaves with white edges.

*Useful Hint*

Small branches of purple leaf plum can be cut in late winter and taken indoors to bloom in a vase in a sunny, warm spot.

# Redbud

*Cercis canadensis*

## A Real Beauty We Often Take for Granted

Redbud is such a familiar tree that many of us tend to take it for granted. But if you enumerate its special traits—heart-shaped leaves, graceful branches, and an abundance of fuchsia flowers before the leaves appear in spring—you realize what a neat native tree this is. It also blooms before dogwoods, so it extends the flowering season in your yard. And it has an almost ethereal glow on gray spring days when it's in full bloom.

## Top Reasons to Plant

- Beautiful, showy spring blooms
- Graceful shape
- Large, heart-shaped leaves in summer
- Small size fits most yards
- Tolerates variety of soil types
- Grows well in partial sun

## Useful Hint

As with dogwoods, keep lawn mowers and string trimmers from damaging the trunk—such damage allows borers and diseases to enter.

76

**Bloom Color**
Pink or white

**Bloom Period**
Spring

**Height/Width**
20 to 35 feet x 25 to 35 feet

**Planting Location**
- Prefers moist, well-drained soil with organic matter but adapts to most soil types, except those that stay wet
- Sun or partial sun

**Planting**
- Plant in spring or early fall.
- Dig the hole as deep as the rootball and twice as wide.
- Place the tree in the hole and water with transplanting solution.
- Fill with dirt removed from the hole.
- Mulch in a circle extending several feet from the trunk.

**Watering**
- Regular water is essential.
- Water when rainfall measures less than an inch in any week during the growing season.

**Fertilizing**
- Fertilize regularly.
- Feed in late fall with 1 to 2 pounds of granular 19-0-0 fertilizer for each inch of trunk diameter or with a high-nitrogen tree fertilizer used according to label directions.

## Easy Tip

Regular watering and fertilizing are the keys to success with redbuds.

**Suggestions for Vigorous Growth**
- Maintain a wide circle of mulch around the trunk to prevent mechanical injury from mowers or trimmers.
- If pruning is needed, do it in winter or after flowering.

**Pest Control**
- Caterpillars may be a problem—control them with Bt (*Bacillus thuringiensis*).

**Complementary Plants**
- Underplant with early-flowering spring bulbs in companionable colors.

**Recommended Selections**
- 'Forest Pansy' has purple leaves in summer.
- 'Royal White' has white flowers.
- 'Tennessee Pink' has clear-pink flowers.

# Red Maple
*Acer rubrum*

## A Beautiful Shade Tree That's Red in Spring and Fall

Do you know why red maple got its name? It's not, as many suppose, because of the fall leaf color. Instead, "red" refers to the abundant flowers in early spring that give the tree a fiery glow. You can't count on unnamed red maples having excellent foliage color, so it's best to buy one of the numerous cultivars developed for the outstanding show they put on in autumn.

## Top Reasons to Plant

○ Red blooms in spring
○ Red foliage in fall
○ Graceful, spreading habit
○ Pest and disease resistant
○ Fast growing
○ Attractive in three seasons
○ Tolerates wet soil

## Useful Hint

Red maple is a relatively fast grower and tolerates wet soil.

**Bloom Color**
Red

**Bloom Period**
Spring

**Height/Width**
40 to 70 feet x 40 to 45 feet

**Planting Location**
- Prefers moist, well-drained, slightly acidic soil, but does well in average soil and wet areas
- Sun

**Planting**
- Plant in late winter or early spring.
- Dig the hole twice as wide as and as deep as the rootball.
- Place the tree in the hole and water with transplanting solution.
- Fill with soil dug from the hole.
- Mulch well.

**Watering**
- This tree needs water spring through fall—water deeply if rainfall doesn't total an inch per week.

**Fertilizing**
- Fertilizer is not usually needed, especially if the tree is growing in a lawn that gets fertilized.

**Suggestions for Vigorous Growth**
- Red maple needs little pruning.

*Easy Tip*

Buy a named cultivar of red maple to ensure you have good fall color.

**Pest Control**
- This tree is occasionally subject to disease, borers (which enter through the trunk), and leafhoppers (which cause the leaves to look mottled and bleached or browned and curled along the edges).
- Knock leafhoppers off with a strong stream of water, and spray young trees with insecticidal soap.

**Complementary Plants**
- Red maple makes an excellent specimen tree placed where it can be seen in spring and fall from indoors or the street.

**Recommended Selections**
- 'October Glory' and 'Red Sunset'® are easy to find and have fabulous fall foliage.
- 'Autumn Blaze' is my current favorite because of its outstanding fall color.

# Red Oak
## *Quercus rubra*

## *A Rapidly Growing Majestic Shade Tree with a Stately Air*

Red oaks are excellent landscape trees that grow quickly and tolerate urban conditions. They mature into symmetrical trees with rounded crowns, adding a majestic touch to the landscape. Tender reddish buds open in spring; during summer, the large pointed leaves are a lustrous dark-green; autumn leaves become deep-red. On older trees, the black, deeply creviced bark adds texture to the landscape.

## Top Reasons to Plant

- Majestic large shade tree
- Grows quickly
- Beautiful fall color
- Tolerates variety of soils
- Easily transplanted
- Pest and disease resistant
- Drought tolerant when established

## *Useful Hint*

A properly planted and cared for red oak grows about 2 feet each year.

## Bloom Color
Grown for its red buds and foliage

## Bloom Period
Buds are showy in spring, foliage in fall.

## Height/Width
75 feet x 35 feet

## Planting Location
- Prefers slightly acidic, sandy loam soils, but tolerates moist clay and dry areas
- Sun

## Planting
- Plant from November through March, preferably a balled-and-burlapped or container-grown tree.
- Dig the hole twice as wide as and the same depth as the rootball.
- Replace up to half the soil in the hole so one-fourth of the rootball is above ground—this helps avoid drainage problems after the soil settles.
- Set the tree in the hole and fill with soil from the hole.
- Water well.
- Mulch with 2 to 3 inches of organic matter.

## Watering
- Water deeply at planting and every ten days during the first growing season.

## Fertilizing
- Feed young trees in late winter to early spring.
- Apply a high-nitrogen fertilizer in spirals beneath the tree beginning 1 foot from the trunk.

## Easy Tip

If you've inherited a white oak (*Quercus alba*) that's in decline due to old age and urban stress, the rapidly growing red oak makes an excellent replacement.

## Suggestions for Vigorous Growth
- Larger specimens may need staking for six months.
- Allow leaves to accumulate under the tree to provide mulch and gentle feeding as they decay.
- Prune only to remove narrow-angled branches and broken twigs.
- Prune trees that have double leaders (twin trunks) to one central trunk.

## Pest Control
- Few pest problems trouble this tree.

## Complementary Plants
- As the tree becomes taller, underplant with shrubs.

## Recommended Selections
- Plant the species.

# River Birch

*Betula nigra*

## A Versatile Tree with Fabulous Bark

When gardeners hear a name like river birch, they naturally assume it's the answer to their search for a tree that doesn't mind clay soil, permanently wet spots, or areas that occasionally flood. And they're right. But that doesn't mean folks with average or drier soils should pass it by. This tree is so versatile—and so good-looking—it belongs in every yard where there's room for it. This cold-hardy, heat-tolerant tree features beautiful peeling bark.

## Top Reasons to Plant

○ Gorgeous peeling bark
○ Graceful shape
○ Grows well in wet clay soil
○ Tolerates variety of growing conditions
○ Disease and pest resistant
○ Good fall color on some cultivars

## Useful Hint

River birch has wonderful peeling bark in shades of salmon and cream—truly stunning year-round.

## Bloom Color
Grown for its foliage and bark

## Height/Width
40 to 70 feet x 40 to 60 feet

## Planting Location
- Prefers moist, acidic soil but adapts to any fertile soil other than alkaline, especially if watered
- Sun or mostly sun

## Planting
- Plant in fall or spring.
- Dig the hole as deep as the rootball and twice as wide.
- Place the tree in the hole and water with transplanting solution.
- Fill with soil from the hole.
- Mulch if soil is on the dry side.

## Watering
- Keep soil moist during the growing season.

## Fertilizing
- Fertilizer is not needed.

## Suggestions for Vigorous Growth
- In dry soils, maintain a 3-inch mulch.
- If necessary, prune in summer—river birch "bleeds" if a branch is cut in spring, which isn't harmful but is messy and discolors the bark.

## Easy Tip
If you like the paperbark birches with white trunks that won't grow here, try river birch instead—you'll be pleased.

## Pest Control
- Few insects or diseases trouble this tree.
- Aphids may appear on tender young growth—hose them off with a hard blast of water and spray with insecticidal soap.

## Complementary Plants
- Many gardeners like the look of a clump of three trees planted together in the same hole.

## Recommended Selections
- 'Heritage' has worked well for me in several places in Tennessee—it's terrific for clay soil, and unlike many river birches, develops pleasing yellow foliage in fall.

# Sassafras

*Sassafras albidum*

## An Outstanding Native Tree for Fall Color

This Tennessee native can't be beat for fall color—its lobed leaves turn to yellow, deep-orange, scarlet, and purple, putting on a stunning show. Its irregular shape—many short, twisted branches that spread to create a broad, flat head at maturity—gives the tree an interesting appearance in winter. In spring, fragrant yellow flowers outline the branches. And in September, female trees bear dark-blue fruits on scarlet stalks that are quite showy if you get to see them before the birds nab them.

## Top Reasons to Plant

○ Showy fall color
○ Fall fruit attracts birds
○ Adapts to variety of conditions
○ Pest and disease resistant
○ Pleasant scent
○ Handsome bark

## Useful Hint

Prune off sucker growth around the base in winter if you want to develop a single-trunked tree.

## Bloom Color
Yellow

## Bloom Period
Spring

## Height/Width
30 to 60 feet x 25 to 40 feet

## Planting Location
- Prefers moist, acidic, well-drained soil, but adapts to a variety of soils
- Sun or partial shade

## Planting
- Plant balled-and-burlapped trees in early spring.
- Dig the hole twice as wide and as deep as the rootball.
- Set the tree in the hole and water with transplanting solution.
- Fill with soil taken from the hole.
- Mulch with 3 inches of shredded bark, fine bark, or pine straw.

## Watering
- Water deeply each week when the tree is young if an inch of rainfall hasn't fallen.
- Once the tree is established, water during dry spells.

## Fertilizing
- No fertilizer is needed.

## Easy Tip

Sassafras has a deep tap root, so it is best planted when the tree is young using container-grown or balled-and-burlapped trees, not dug from the wild.

## Suggestions for Vigorous Growth
- Prune as needed in winter.
- Sucker growth tends to form, especially if roots are damaged by cultivation.
- Keep mulched year-round.
- If leaves turn yellowish in summer, it likely means chlorosis from soil that is not acidic enough—feed with fertilizer made for acid-loving trees.

## Pest Control
- No serious pests or diseases trouble this tree.

## Complementary Plants
- Combine with other natives in naturalized plantings.

## Recommended Selections
- Plant the species.

# Saucer Magnolia
*Magnolia × soulangiana*

## A Spring Knockout with Big, Bold Blooms

When you buy a small tree, it's sometimes tough knowing you'll have to wait several years before you can enjoy its flowers. But there's not likely to be much delay before saucer magnolia begins flowering. It's often covered with full-sized pink and white or purplish flowers when only 3 feet tall. Although saucer magnolia can be trained as a large shrub, I think it's more effective in the landscape as a tree.

## Top Reasons to Plant

○ Showy spring blooms
○ Graceful shape
○ Attractive in winter
○ Disease and pest resistant
○ Can be trained as tree or multitrunked shrub
○ Fragrant flowers

**Bloom Color**
Pink, purplish, or white

**Bloom Period**
Early spring

**Height/Width**
10 to 30 feet x 15 to 20 feet

**Planting Location**
- Moist, well-drained, acidic soil containing organic matter
- Sun

**Planting**
- Plant in spring.
- Dig the hole as deep as the rootball and twice as wide.
- Place the tree in the hole and water with transplanting solution.
- Fill with soil from the hole.
- Mulch with pine straw or fine bark.

**Watering**
- Water deeply whenever rainfall has been less than an inch in any week.

**Fertilizing**
- No fertilizer is needed.

## Easy Tip

If you're impatient, this is the flowering tree for you—it typically has full-sized blossoms when it's very small.

**Suggestions for Vigorous Growth**
- Maintain year-round mulch to keep soil moist.
- Prune just after flowering, if needed, to develop a tree form—one trunk with four or five main branches starting a foot above ground level.

**Pest Control**
- Few insects and diseases trouble this tree.

**Complementary Plants**
- Choose several of these trees with varying flower colors and place them in different areas of the yard.

**Recommended Selections**
- 'Alba' features fragrant, white flowers.
- 'Rustica Rubra' has large reddish purple blooms and red seedpods.

## Useful Hint

Mother Nature can be your enemy with this tree—causing unseasonably warm weather that encourages blooming followed by a hard frost that kills the flowers.

# Serviceberry

*Amelanchier* species and hybrids

## A Graceful Small Tree with Flowers and More

Like many native plants, serviceberry has collected a number of common names. My mom always called it sarvis tree. Other people call it Juneberry for the dark little fruits in early summer (supposedly sweet and good for cooking—I wouldn't know, as the birds always get mine). Serviceberry has clusters of white flowers in early spring. They're fleeting, but to me, they're the sign that spring has truly sprung.

## Top Reasons to Plant

- Beautiful flowers in spring
- Fruit that attracts birds
- Graceful, airy form
- Grows moderately fast
- Few insects or diseases
- Excellent fall color
- Grass grows underneath

## Useful Hint

*Amelanchier arborea* is the tree species most commonly available to gardeners, although Allegheny serviceberry (*Amelanchier laevis*) is often found in the wild.

**Bloom Color**
White

**Bloom Period**
Early spring

**Height/Width**
15 to 30 feet x 20 to 30 feet

**Planting Location**
- Prefers moist, acidic, well-drained soil, but tolerates many soil types
- Sun or partial shade

**Planting**
- Plant container-grown or balled-and-burlapped trees in spring or fall.
- Dig the hole twice as wide as and as deep as the rootball.
- Place the tree at the same depth it grew before.
- Fill hole with soil removed from it.
- Water well.
- Mulch.

**Watering**
- In early years, water in those weeks when there isn't an inch of rainfall.
- Established trees should cope with mild dry spells.
- Water deeply during droughts.

**Fertilizing**
- Fertilizer is not usually needed.

## Easy Tip

Pay attention to serviceberry's eventual spread if you decide to grow it as a multistemmed shrub rather than a tree—it takes a lot of room.

**Suggestions for Vigorous Growth**
- If pruning is needed, do it in spring after blooming has finished.
- Maintain mulch year-round, especially in dry weather.

**Pest Control**
- Few insects or diseases trouble this tree.

**Complementary Plants**
- Plant with spring wildflowers along the edge of woods.
- Pair it with shadbush (*Amelanchier canadensis*), a shrub form with excellent fall color.

**Recommended Selections**
- *Amelanchier grandiflora* 'Autumn Brilliance' has very red fall foliage and grows fast.
- 'Princess Diana' displays spectacular red leaves in fall.

# Sourwood

*Oxydendrum arboreum*

### *An Easy-to-Grow Native That Looks Exotic and Unusual*

Sourwood has such an unusual exotic appearance that it's easy to imagine it was discovered in some remote place on the other side of the world. Instead, it's an easy-to-grow native that most of us take for granted. Sourwood calls attention to its beauty with 10-inch clusters of creamy, bell-shaped flowers in summer, followed in autumn by ivory seed capsules that hang from the tips of the branches and by brilliant scarlet foliage.

## Top Reasons to Plant

○ Long clusters of creamy flowers in summer
○ Strands of ivory seed capsules in fall
○ Brilliant scarlet fall color
○ Attractive pyramidal shape
○ Few pests and diseases
○ Needs little care

## Useful Hint

Although sourwood tolerates some shade, its blooms and fall color are much better in full sun.

**Bloom Color**
Cream

**Bloom Period**
Summer

**Height/Width**
25 to 50 feet x 15 to 20 feet

**Planting Location**
• Acidic, well-drained soil
• Sun

**Planting**
• Plant in a prominent spot in early fall or spring.
• Dig the hole as deep as the rootball and twice as wide.
• Fill hole with soil removed from it.
• Water with transplant solution.
• Mulch well with pine straw or shredded leaves, but don't let the mulch touch the trunk.

**Watering**
• When the tree is young, water well during dry spells.
• Once mature, sourwood can tolerate some dryness.
• Water small- and medium-sized trees during droughts.

*Easy Tip*

Sourwood blooms at a time when few other trees do.

**Fertilizing**
• Fertilizer is not needed unless the tree is not growing well.
• If necessary, apply high-nitrogen tree fertilizer in autumn after leaves have fallen.

**Suggestions for Vigorous Growth**
• Little pruning is needed.
• Slow growth is normal.

**Pest Control**
• Few serious insects or diseases bother this tree.

**Complementary Plants**
• Plant sourwood in a place where it can show off its exotic looks and early autumn color.
• Use against an evergreen backdrop.

**Recommended Selections**
• 'Chameleon' is a kaleidoscope of fall color with leaves turning from green to yellow, red, and purple, often with all colors at once.

# Southern Magnolia
*Magnolia grandiflora*

## The Quintessential Southern Belle of Trees

No tree is more identified with the South than southern magnolia. In fact, most of us simply call this beautiful evergreen "magnolia." Don't let minor objections keep you from owning a true grande dame. There are dwarf cultivars for people who think the tree grows too big and cold-hardy cultivars for those who live in the mountains. So there's really no reason any Tennessee yard should be without this spectacular native.

## Top Reasons to Plant

- Huge creamy-white blossoms
- Fragrant flowers
- Shiny evergreen foliage
- Attractive seedpods with red seeds
- Few pests and diseases
- Good cut flower
- Good cut foliage for winter holiday decorations

**Bloom Color**
White

**Bloom Period**
Late spring and early summer

**Height/Width**
20 to 80 feet x 20 to 50 feet

**Planting Location**
• Rich, moist, acidic, well-drained soil
• Sun
• Protected from winter winds, if possible

**Planting**
• Plant in early spring.
• Dig the hole twice as wide as and as deep as the rootball.
• Set the tree in the hole and fill the hole with soil dug from it.
• Water well.
• Mulch well with organic matter.

**Watering**
• Water deeply when rainfall is below normal.

**Fertilizing**
• Fertilizer is not needed, but for faster growth, spread high-nitrogen tree fertilizer beneath the limbs in late fall.

## Easy Tip
Cut the white flowers and float them in a shallow bowl of water.

**Suggestions for Vigorous Growth**
• Prune in early spring if needed.
• Leave lower limbs to preserve the tree's graceful look and to hide its debris.

**Pest Control**
• Few insect or disease problems bother this tree.

**Complementary Plants**
• Southern magnolia makes a handsome specimen tree.
• Use for screening—they're attractive year-round and, with regular water and fertilizer, grow much faster than you might expect.

**Recommended Selections**
• Beautiful 'Bracken's Brown Beauty' is very cold hardy.
• 'Edith Bogue' is also cold hardy and least likely to suffer snow damage.
• 'Little Gem' grows about 20 to 25 feet tall and 10 to 15 feet wide, and its smaller leaves are nice in arrangements.
• 'Riegel' is also small but with large flowers.
• 'Spring Hill' has a columnar growing habit.

## Useful Hint
The solution to the "messiness" of old leaves and seedpods is to plant the southern magnolia in a mulched bed (not the lawn) and never remove the lower limbs—the trash just disappears.

# Sugar Maple
*Acer saccharum*

*A Wonderful Large Shade Tree with Spectacular Fall Color*

Of all the maples in the colder parts of Tennessee, none produces more wonderful fall color than the sugar maple. With plenty of room to mature, a sugar maple is almost unsurpassable as a shade tree. It definitely is not for the courtyard or small residential property. This maple has dull-green leaves in summer that turn to gorgeous orange and yellow with the first frosts. It grows more slowly than the red maple, but it has a beautiful symmetrical form.

## Top Reasons to Plant

- Stunning fall foliage
- Beautiful form
- Strong branches
- Excellent shade tree
- Needs little care
- Few pests and diseases

## Useful Hint

The strong branches of sugar maple hold up well in ice storms.

### Bloom Color
Grown primarily for its foliage

### Bloom Period
Foliage is effective in fall

### Height/Width
60+ feet x 40 feet

### Planting Location
- Best in moist, fertile, well-drained soil, but tolerates wide range of conditions
- Sun

### Planting
- Plant balled-and-burlapped trees in late winter and container-grown trees in spring or early fall.
- Dig the hole twice the width of and the same depth as the rootball.
- Set the tree in the hole and water with transplanting solution.
- Fill with soil dug from the hole.
- Water well.
- Mulch well.

### Watering
- For the first six weeks, water twice each week if there's little rainfall.
- Thereafter, water during August and September if weekly rainfall is less than an inch.

### Fertilizing
- Fertilizer is not necessary as long as leaves remain a rich green.

## Easy Tip
This is not a tree for small properties—unless you have room to let it grow properly, choose a smaller tree.

- After the first full growing season, feed with slow-release fertilizer in spring at the rate of 1 pound for each inch of trunk diameter.
- Do not fertilize again for two or three years.

### Suggestions for Vigorous Growth
- Remove any shoots rising off the trunk.
- Remove crowded branches from young trees.
- In late summer, limb up (prune away lower limbs) trees growing in lawns.

### Pest Control
- Maple worms and aphids may appear but aren't serious.

### Complementary Plants
- Sugar maple makes an excellent specimen tree in a large yard.
- Use it to line a long, wide driveway.

### Recommended Selections
- 'Green Mountain'® tolerates hot sites without scorching.
- 'Legacy' is a good, new cultivar.

# Sweet Bay Magnolia

*Magnolia virginiana*

## A Smaller, Moisture-Loving Cousin of Southern Magnolia

Nothing beats the smell of magnolias blooming during late spring and summer. And unlike southern magnolia, sweet bay magnolia blends into the landscape. It works well as a patio tree or in other limited spaces where you want an ornamental tree with a delightful fragrance. Deciduous in cold areas, sweet bay is mostly evergreen in warm areas. It does well in swampy, wet soils, and even allows turf to grow beneath its branches.

## Top Reasons to Plant

- Beautiful creamy-white flowers
- Fragrant blossoms
- Much smaller than southern magnolia
- Good for small yards and gardens
- Tolerates wet soil
- Attractive seedpods
- Good cut flowers

## Useful Hint

Sweet bay is a possiblet substitute for southern magnolia in smaller yards where soil is moist or watering easy.

## Bloom Color
Creamy-white

## Bloom Period
Spring to summer

## Height/Width
20 to 40 feet x 15 to 25 feet

## Planting Location
- Best in moist, fertile soil
- Sun, with some shade in the hottest part of the day

## Planting
- Plant in early fall or spring.
- Dig the hole twice as wide as and the same depth as the rootball.
- Place the tree in the hole and fill the hole with original dirt.
- Water well and apply a transplant solution.
- Mulch with 2 to 3 inches of fine pine bark or other organic matter.

## Watering
- Water regularly and do not let the soil dry out—sweet bay does not tolerate drought.

## Easy Tip
Consistently moist soil is the key to success with sweet bay magnolia—its other common name is swamp magnolia.

## Fertilizing
- Feed in late fall or spring with a slow-release, granular azalea fertilizer.

## Suggestions for Vigorous Growth
- Prune only if necessary or to remove dead or damaged branches.

## Pest Control
- No significant pests or diseases bother this tree.

## Complementary Plants
- Plant among azaleas.
- Use in a ground-cover bed or with low-growing shrubs.

## Recommended Selections
- Plant the species.

# Sweet Gum
*Liquidambar styraciflua*

## A Shade Tree with Leaves Beautiful in Summer and Fall

Sweet gum is beloved by kindergarten teachers and crafters and muttered over by those who have to mow the lawn. It's admired for the shape of its deep-green leaves and their impressive reddish purple fall color. By placing the tree on the sunny edge of woods or in an island bed, I steer clear of aggravation while enjoying some of the best and longest-lasting fall color.

## Top Reasons to Plant

- Beautiful red leaves in fall
- Attractive, unusual shape to leaves
- Excellent shade tree for large area
- Thrives in wet soil
- Few pests or diseases

## Useful Hint

If you want to plant a sweet gum but don't want the nuisance of the sticky balls, go for one of the "ball-less" cultivars—'Cherokee'® and 'Rotundiloba' are both good selections.

## Height/Width
60 to 75 feet x 30 to 45 feet

## Planting Location
- Best in moist or wet, acidic soils (leaves yellow in alkaline soils)
- Sun

## Planting
- Plant in spring.
- Dig the hole as deep as and twice as wide as the rootball.
- Place the tree in the hole and fill with soil from the hole.
- Water well.
- Mulch.

## Watering
- Keep the soil moist until the tree begins growing well—probably within a year or two.
- After the tree becomes established, water whenever weekly total rainfall is less than an inch.

## Fertilizing
- During the second year after planting, in late autumn, spread 1 pound of granular 19-0-0 fertilizer for each inch of trunk diameter in a wide circle beneath the limbs.

## Easy Tip

This is not a tree for small yards, so think carefully before choosing sweet gum.

## Suggestions for Vigorous Growth
- Do any required pruning in winter.

## Pest Control
- Caterpillars or scale may appear—use *Bacillus thuringiensis* (Bt) for caterpillars and a light horticultural oil (sometimes called sun oil) to smother scale.

## Complementary Plants
- If one is a standout, two or three together in a small grove are dazzling.

## Recommended Selections
- 'Cherokee'® and 'Rotundiloba' generally do not produce the balls for which sweet gum is famous.
- 'Palo Alto' has a reddish orange fall color.

# Thornless Honey Locust

*Gleditsia triacanthos* f. *inermis*

*A Fine-Textured, Adaptable Tree with Light, Airy Foliage*

Their drought resistance and adaptability to a range of suburban and city conditions account for the huge popularity of the honey locust as a yard specimen. Breeders have developed a thornless version with nice proportions and light, airy foliage. Featuring twenty to thirty small leaflets, the green leaves turn pale-yellow in autumn. In early summer, the scented flowers bloom an inconspicuous green, then give way to 8-inch-long pods later in the summer—unless you choose a type that has no pods.

## Top Reasons to Plant

- Lovely, fine-textured foliage
- Nice fall color
- Drought tolerant when established
- Grass grows beneath branches
- Thrives in any well-drained soil

## Useful Hint

Be sure to choose a variety of honey locust with no thorns or pods.

**Bloom Color**
Inconspicuous green flowers

**Bloom Period**
Spring

**Height/Width**
30 to 50 feet x 30 feet

**Planting Location**
• Not fussy as to soil type as long as the soil is well drained
• Sun

**Planting**
• Plant balled-and-burlapped trees in spring and container-grown ones anytime during the growing season.
• Dig the hole as deep as and twice as wide as the rootball.
• Place the tree in the hole so the top of the rootball is at soil level.
• Fill with soil from the hole.
• Shape remaining soil into a saucer to hold water around the tree.
• Water well.
• Mulch with 2 to 3 inches of organic matter.

**Watering**
• Water regularly until established.

**Fertilizing**
• No fertilizer is needed.

*Easy Tip*

The airy, fine-textured foliage of honey locust permits grass to thrive under its branches.

**Suggestions for Vigorous Growth**
• Maintain mulch year-round to keep soil moist and to reduce weeds.

**Pest Control**
• Webworms (caterpillars) may appear— prune out their nests.

**Complementary Plants**
• Thornless honey locust makes an excellent specimen tree in an open spot in the lawn.
• Plant along fence lines or property boundaries to be viewed from the house.

**Recommended Selections**
• Cultivars with no seedpods or thorns include 'Halka'™, which is compact and rounded; 'Moraine', with deep-green foliage turning yellow in fall; 'Shademaster'®, which has a good form with ascending branches; and 'Sunburst', with golden spring foliage.

# Tulip Poplar

*Liriodendron tulipifera*

## A Beauty That Is Tennessee's Official State Tree

The beautiful tulip poplar certainly deserves its status as the official tree of Tennessee. It's tall and majestic, the flowers are mildly fragrant, and the leaves turn yellow in autumn. But there's one problem—tiny tulip poplar tree seedlings are often given away to homeowners who have no clue how large they grow. This is one of our biggest native trees, suitable mostly for large properties.

## Top Reasons to Plant

○ Tall, majestic tree for large areas
○ Beautiful blooms
○ Fragrant flowers
○ Distinctive leaf shape
○ Good fall color

## Useful Hint

If tulip poplar is a favorite of yours, but you have a small yard, look for some of the smaller cultivars now becoming available at nurseries.

## Bloom Color
Cream to yellow

## Bloom Period
Late spring to early summer

## Height/Width
70 to 100 feet x 35 to 55 feet

## Planting Location
• Moist, well-drained, slightly acidic soil
• Sun

## Planting
• Plant in spring.
• Dig the hole as deep as the rootball and twice as wide.
• Place the tree in the hole and fill with original dirt.
• Water with transplanting solution.
• Mulch well with organic matter such as pine straw or shredded leaves.

## Watering
• Moisture is essential—without it, leaves scorch and drop.
• Keep soil moist at all times, especially when the tree is young and during dry weather.

## Fertilizing
• Do not fertilize unless the tree is not growing well.

*Easy Tip*

Place tulip poplar where it has plenty of room to grow—well away from power lines and buildings.

## Suggestions for Vigorous Growth
• Ensure that the soil receives adequate, regular moisture.

## Pest Control
• Numerous insect and disease problems plague this tree.
• Aphids are common, producing a sweet secretion often followed by black sooty mold—use a hose-end sprayer to wash off the mold, then spray the tree with insecticidal soap or light horticultural oil to get rid of the aphids.

## Complementary Plants
• Tulip poplar makes an excellent specimen tree; plant where it can be admired and has room to grow.

## Recommended Selections
• Smaller cultivars include 'Ardis' and 'Compactum'.

# Willow Oak

*Quercus phellos*

## A Popular, Fast-Growing Tree with Few Problems

Willow oak is an excellent landscape tree that has virtually no disease problems. It grows rapidly, tolerating urban conditions so well that it is widely used as a street tree in cities and towns. It withstands Tennessee summers with little effort, and its graceful willowlike foliage is always fresh and green. It's easy to transplant and grows 2 to 3 feet per year once established, reaching a respectable size in a decade or less. It's also a good tree on which to hang the hammock.

## Top Reasons to Plant

- Attractive, willowlike leaves
- Golden-bronze foliage in fall
- Grows quickly
- Few pests and diseases
- Tolerates polluted air

## Useful Hint

These aren't trees for small yards, so if you don't really have room for a willow oak, select another tree.

## Height/Width
80 feet x 75 feet

## Planting Location
- Prefers slightly acidic, moist, loamy soil
- Sun or partial sun

## Planting
- Smaller trees transplant more successfully than large ones.
- Plant balled-and-burlapped or container-grown trees in late winter or spring.
- Dig the hole twice as wide as and as deep as the rootball.
- Place the tree in the hole and fill the hole with soil.
- Water well.
- Mulch.

## Watering
- Water regularly the first year or two.

## Fertilizing
- Fertilize in spring of the second year as buds begin to swell.

## Suggestions for Vigorous Growth
- Keep mulched in a 4-foot ring starting 6 inches from the trunk.
- Stake top-heavy trees for four to six months.

## Easy Tip
If you like the look of willow trees, plant willow oak instead—the foliage is similar, but willow oak does not have the problems that willow trees do.

- Protect the trunk from mower or string-trimmer damage.
- As the tree grows, remove branches with narrow crotches and forking upright branches.

## Pest Control
- The major pest is the orange-striped oakworm, which can be annoying but does little long-term damage.

## Complementary Plants
- Willow oak makes an excellent specimen shade tree.

## Recommended Selections
- Plant the species.

# Winter King Hawthorn
*Crataegus viridis* 'Winter King'

## A Beautiful Small Tree with Spring Blooms, Fall Color, and Winter Fruit

'Winter King' overcomes the typical fungus diseases suffered by hawthorns. It has a broad vase shape and bears clusters of delicate white flowers in spring. After a show of bronze, red, and gold fall foliage, it reveals silvery bark patched with orange-brown and develops orange-red fruits that persist through winter. Hawthorns are famous for their thorns, but 'Winter King' has sparse, small ones.

## Top Reasons to Plant

- Lovely branching structure
- Nice bark
- Beautiful white spring blooms
- Outstanding fall foliage
- Red fruits that last through winter
- Few pests and diseases
- Tolerates many soil types

## Useful Hint

Plant 'Winter King' where it can be viewed from inside during winter, when its bark and red fruits really show off.

**Bloom Color**
White

**Bloom Period**
Spring

**Height/Width**
20 to 30 feet x 20 to 30 feet

**Planting Location**
- Tolerates any soil but appreciates rich, deep soil
- Sun is best but tolerates some shade

**Planting**
- Plant in spring.
- Dig the hole twice as wide as and as deep as the rootball.
- Set the tree in the hole so the rootball is level with the ground.
- Fill the hole with soil dug from it.
- Form a saucer with the soil to hold water.
- Water well.
- Mulch with 2 or 3 inches of organic material.

**Watering**
- Water new trees during the first year or two when rainfall is scarce.

**Fertilizing**
- No fertilizer is needed if mulch is maintained year-round to decay and gently feed the tree.

**Suggestions for Vigorous Growth**
- Keep mulched year-round to hold soil moisture.
- Young trees exposed to wind may need temporary staking.

*Easy Tip*

Hawthorns are generally subject to a number of serious diseases, so stick to 'Winter King' if you want to plant a hawthorn.

- Prune off all suckers promptly—'Winter King' is grafted onto the rootstock of the Washington hawthorn, and suckers develop below the graft.
- Prune off any water sprouts (weak, suckering shoots) along branches.

**Pest Control**
- Caterpillars, scale, or borers may attack stressed trees, so ensure 'Winter King' receives adequate water.

**Complementary Plants**
- 'Winter King' is best used as a specimen tree—site it to be viewed from indoors and where it has plenty of room to spread and show its beautiful shape.

**Recommended Selections**
- Washington hawthorn (*Crataegus phaenopyrum*), on whose roots 'Winter King' is grafted, is itself disease resistant and very attractive, but it has thorns 1 to 3 inches long and is not suitable where there are children.

# Yellowwood
*Cladastris kentukea*

## A Gorgeous Spring-Bloomer with Fall and Winter Assets

If you drive Tennessee highways, you've probably admired this tree's long clusters of creamy flowers and wondered what vine or tree was growing along the roadside. The flowers alone are reason enough to grow yellowwood, but it brings other fine qualities to the landscape—bright-green leaves in summer that turn yellow in fall, smooth gray bark that adds winter interest, an ability to grow in alkaline soil, and extreme winter hardiness.

## Top Reasons to Plant

- Pretty spring blooms
- Good fall color
- Nice winter bark
- Tolerates wide variety of soils
- Very winter hardy
- No serious pests or diseases

## Useful Hint

Yellowwood is a nice patio or terrace tree due to its relatively small scale.

**Bloom Color**
White or pink

**Bloom Period**
Late spring

**Height/Width**
30 to 60 feet x 40 to 50 feet

**Planting Location**
- Well-drained acidic or alkaline soil
- Sun

**Planting**
- Plant in spring.
- Dig the hole twice as wide as and as deep as the rootball.
- Place the tree in the hole and water with transplanting solution.
- Fill the hole with soil dug from it.

**Watering**
- Regular watering promotes faster growth.
- Keep soil moist while the tree is young.
- As the tree ages, water when rainfall hasn't totaled an inch per week— though yellowwood tolerates some dryness.

**Fertilizing**
- Fertilizing promotes faster growth.
- Feed with 1 pound of granular 19-0-0 fertilizer per inch of trunk diameter in late autumn.

## Easy Tip

Once established, yellowwood can tolerate some drought.

**Suggestions for Vigorous Growth**
- When the tree is young, remove limbs with narrow crotches (limbs that join the trunk at a narrow angle rather than a wide one).
- Prune storm damage as soon as possible after it occurs.
- Do all other pruning in summer—in spring, this tree "bleeds" sap, which is messy and disturbing to watch, although not harmful.

**Pest Control**
- No significant pests or diseases trouble this tree.

**Complementary Plants**
- Grow as a shade tree or a lawn specimen.

**Recommended Selections**
- 'Rosea' has fragrant, light-pink flowers.

# Yoshino Cherry

*Prunus × yedoensis*

## A Spectacular Flowering Cherry Like a Luminous White Cloud

Yoshino cherry is another of the spectacular flowering cherries brought over from Japan in the early 1900s. In spring, abundant white flowers cover the ends of the branches, appearing before the leaves do. Yoshino cherry flowers are fragrant, smelling slightly of almonds. This is the cherry that surrounds the Tidal Basin in Washington, D.C.—some years actually blooming during the Cherry Blossom Festival.

## Top Reasons to Plant

- Gorgeous spring blooms
- Good fragrant cut flowers
- Graceful branching habit
- Relatively small size
- Nice fall color on some cultivars

## Useful Hint

Yoshino cherries are propagated either by rooting small cuttings or by grafting a cutting onto another cherry trunk. Since the lower cherry rootstock can send up sprouts quite unlike the Yoshino, it is best to buy trees produced by rooted cuttings.

## Bloom Color
White or pale-pink

## Bloom Period
Spring

## Height/Width
20 to 30 feet x 25 to 40 feet

## Planting Location
- Fertile, well-drained soil with organic matter
- In poorly drained clay soils, consider planting on mounds or in raised beds
- Sun

## Planting
- Plant in spring or early autumn.
- Dig the hole as deep as the rootball and twice as wide.
- Place the tree in the hole and water with transplanting solution.
- Fill with soil dug from the hole.
- Water well.
- Mulch with 2 to 3 inches of pine straw.

## Watering
- Water when rainfall is less than an inch per week.
- To avoid root rot, be careful not to overwater in clay soil.

## Fertilizing
- Feed in late fall with a high-nitrogen fertilizer for trees, used according to label directions.

*Easy Tip*

If a young tree needs support, stake it for six months to a year.

## Suggestions for Vigorous Growth
- Prune if needed as soon as flowers fade.
- Maintain mulch to protect the trunk from damage by lawn equipment.

## Pest Control
- Tent caterpillars may be a problem.
- Flowering cherries are subject to several pests and diseases—if any appear, consult the Extension Service for causes and cures.

## Complementary Plants
- Plant with azaleas, rhododendrons, and nearby dogwoods.
- Underplant Yoshino cherry with white or pale-pink spring bulbs.

## Recommended Selections
- 'Cascade Snow'™ has white flowers, dark-green leaves in summer that turn orangish in fall, and fewer disease problems than most flowering cherries.
- 'Royal Burgundy' features foliage that is reddish purple when new and reddish orange in fall.

# Gardening Basics

Gardening isn't difficult; even small children are successful gardeners. But, as with other hobbies, gardening requires paying attention to the basics—soil, water, fertilizer, mulch, and weather. Pay attention to those, and you'll have a landscape to be proud of. Here's what you need to know.

## *Soil*

### Soil Is the Foundation

It's hard to get excited about dirt. It's not as interesting as plants. It doesn't bloom; it just sits there, underfoot. But the soil is the foundation for all your gardening. If the soil is good (either naturally or you've improved it), then plants are going to be happy. If the soil is poor, plants won't grow well and will develop problems.

So the first step is to learn what your soil is like. Your nearby neighbors can probably tell you; so can the Soil Conservation Service office in your county. A simple home test is to pick up a golf-ball-sized piece of moist but not wet soil. Squeeze and then release it. If the ball of soil crumbles, it has a balanced texture. If it holds its shape, it's clay.

### The Importance of the Right Conditions

If you've read about gardening at all, you've heard the advice about having your soil tested. That's wise counsel. All it involves is digging up small samples of soil from various parts of your yard, mixing them together well, and turning them in to your County Extension Service to be sent off for testing. The best time to do this is fall, when the labs aren't so busy and when—if your soil needs lime—there's plenty of time to apply it and for it to begin to take effect.

When your soil test results come back, you'll learn if your soil is deficient in any nutrients (and consequently what kind and how much fertilizer to use) and also the pH of your soil. What's pH? It's the measure of acidity or alkalinity of your soil. A pH of 7 is neutral—below that is acidic, above that is alkaline. In Tennessee, most of our soils are acidic, but some of us do live on properties with alkaline soil. Because plants have definite preferences for one type or the other, it's important to know your soil's pH level.

Because the ideal soil for most plants is moist and well drained, it's good to know whether your soil tends to stay wet or dry and whether it drains well. Clay soils stay wet longer than loam; sandy or rocky soils drain much faster than other types of soil—which is often good—but they need watering more frequently. Plants that are able to live in especially wet or dry conditions are noted in the descriptions throughout this book.

If you suspect that drainage is poor at a site in your yard, test to be sure. Dig a hole 6 to 12 inches deep and as wide. Fill the hole with water and time how long it takes for the water to drain completely. If it takes

15 minutes to half an hour, drainage is good. Faster means the soil doesn't hold moisture well, and slower means clay.

### Improving Your Soil

Just because your yard has a particular type of soil doesn't mean you have to live with it. Instead, improve it with soil amendments. Organic matter, such as compost, not only lightens heavy clay soil and improves its drainage, but it also boosts the water-holding capability of lighter soil.

Other good soil amendments include rotted leaves, rotted sawdust, composted manure, fine bark, old mushroom compost, and peat moss.

If you're digging a new bed, spread 3 or more inches of compost or other soil amendment on top of the soil and till it into the top 8 inches of soil. Otherwise, improve the soil as you plant.

# Water

### How Much Is Enough?

The rule of thumb says most popular garden plants need 1 inch of water per week in the growing season, and many need its equivalent all year long. Unfortunately, the amount of rain that fell at your city's airport, or other official weather station, may not be the amount that fell on your plants. The only way to know for sure is to put up a rain gauge to assist in obtaining a specific measurement. In summer, when "scattered showers" are always in the forecast, I find that the "official" rainfall and what fell on my yard are rarely the same. If I had watered—or not watered—on the basis of the totals given by the National Weather Service, I would almost always either overwater or under-water my plants. Instead, I save time and money—as well as protect my plants—by knowing exactly how much rainfall they receive.

### When and How to Water

In general, plants respond best to thorough but occasional soakings rather than daily spurts of smaller amounts of water. Regulate water pressure to reduce runoff so more water gets into the soil. Such good garden practices as these encourage plants to develop deeper roots, which provide greater stability; that's especially important for shrubs and trees. Deep roots also make plants more drought-tolerant.

The worst thing you can do for your plants in a drought is to stand over them with a hose for a few minutes each evening. Most of the water runs off instead of soaking in, and what does penetrate the soil doesn't usually go deeply enough. The soil should be wet to at least 8 to 10 inches deep for perennials and other flowers; 12 to 24 inches deep for trees and shrubs. Insert a dry stick into the soil to be sure how far the water has penetrated. It's impossible to say how long watering will take, because water absorption rates vary by soil type. An inch of water will penetrate fastest into sandy soil and slowest into clay. Time your watering the first few times and then you'll have a guide for future watering.

If you use sprinklers or an irrigation system, set out coffee cans at intervals to measure the amount of water delivered in 30 minutes. That will show you how long it will take the system to deliver an inch of water to your plants.

Too little water causes plants to perform poorly. Small leaves, pale or no flowers, stunted size, wilting, little or no fruit formation, and premature leaf drop can all be signs of water stress. Soil surfaces may dry out and even crack, destroying feeder roots near the surface; their loss can be fatal to annual flowers and vegetables. If watering seems adequate and plants still wilt daily, they may be located in too much sun. If such beds are deeply mulched, check to be certain that the water is getting down into the soil.

The best time of day to water is early morning; late afternoon is second best. No one wants to get up at 4 a.m. to turn on a lawn sprinkler. But there's an easy way out. Water timers can be attached to any hose and faucet to regulate sprinklers and soaker hoses; their effective use is the hallmark of in-ground irrigation systems. Soaker hoses—which don't wet foliage—may be used any time day or night.

## The Right Tools

As with all gardening activities, watering is more efficient with the right equipment. Small gardens and containers of plants can be watered efficiently with only a garden hose and watering can—use a water-breaking nozzle to convert the solid stream of water into smaller droplets that will not damage plants. When watering container plants, irrigate until water flows out the drain hole in the bottom of the pot, and then cover the soil with water once again. This practice keeps the root zone healthy by exchanging gases in the soil.

Larger garden beds require sprinklers, either portable or in-ground systems. Sprinklers spread plenty of water around and most of it gets to soil level; the rest is lost to evaporation but does provide a playground and essential moisture for birds. Adjustable sprinkler heads are a good investment; the ability to set the pattern specifically to increase the size of the water droplets gives the gardener more control over irrigation.

Where water is precious or pricey, drip watering systems and soaker hoses offer very efficient irrigation. They're especially useful around plants, such as roses and zinnias, that develop mildew or other fungus diseases easily. These hoses apply much smaller amounts of water at one time than you may be used to. To measure output, let the water run for an hour, then turn the soaker hose off. Dig down into the soil to see how deeply it is wet. That will help you gauge how long to keep soaker hoses or drip systems on. For the health of your plants, when watering this way, occasionally supplement with overhead watering (either sprinklers or hand-held hoses) to clean the leaves and deter insects.

### Watering Plants in Containers

Because hanging baskets and annuals in small pots often become rootbound by midsummer—when temperature and humidity levels are high—they may need watering once or even twice daily. You can lessen this chore slightly by mixing a super-absorbent polymer into the soil at planting time. When mixed, these look like Jell-O®. They absorb moisture, and then release it as the plants need it. Although they're pricey, only a tiny amount is needed (never use more than what is recommended, or you'll have a mess on your hands), and they last in the soil for up to five years. My experience is that they just about double the length of time between waterings. That is, if I would water a container plant without the polymer once a day, then with the polymer, I can usually water every other day. That may not sound like a big deal, but in the dog days of August it's a blessing! These super-absorbent polymers are sold under a number of trade names; ask for them at garden centers and nurseries.

### Why Is Watering Important?

Water is vital because it makes up at least 95 percent of a plant's mass, and its timely supply is crucial to healthy growth. It is literally the elixir of life, moving from the root zone and leaf surfaces into the plant's systems, carrying nutrients and filling cells to create stems, leaves, flowers, and fruit. Without ample water for roots to work efficiently, nutrients go unabsorbed, growth is stunted, and plant tissues eventually collapse, wilt, and die. Ironically, too much water creates equally disastrous conditions. When soils are flooded, the roots suffocate, stop pumping water and nutrients, and the plant eventually dies.

### Watering Tips

- Shrubs and other plants growing under the overhang of the roof may need more frequent watering than those planted out in the yard. Foundation shrubs often don't get much water from precipitation, and they also have to contend with the reflected heat from the house.
- Raised beds, berms, and mounds also need watering more often.
- Watch out for excessive runoff when watering. If the soil isn't absorbing the moisture, slow down the rate of water application.
- Never fertilize without watering thoroughly afterward. Fertilizer salts can damage the roots if moisture is lacking.

## *Fertilizer*

Nutrition in appropriate amounts is as important as sunlight and water to plant growth. Three elements—nitrogen, phosphorus, and potassium—

are essential to plants and are called macronutrients. Some of these nutrients are obtained from the soil, but if they're not available in the amounts needed, the gardener must provide them through fertilizer.

## The Role of Nutrition

Each nutrient plays a major role in plant development. Nitrogen produces healthy, green leaves, while phosphorus and potassium are responsible for strong stems, flowers, and fruit. Without enough of any one of the macronutrients, plants falter and often die. Other elements, needed in much smaller amounts, are known as *trace elements, minor elements,* or *micronutrients.* Included in most complete fertilizers, the minor elements are boron, iron, manganese, zinc, copper, and molybdenum.

Fertilizers come from two basic sources: organic materials and manufactured ones. Organic sources include rocks, plants, and animals; fertilizers are extracted or composted from them. The advantages of organics affect both plants and people: centuries of history to explain their uses, slow and steady action on plants and especially soils, and the opportunity to put local and recycled materials to good use. Manufactured sources are the products of laboratories. Nutrients are formulated by scientists and produced in factories. The advantages of commercially prepared inorganic fertilizers are consistency of product, formula diversity, definitive analysis of contents, and ready availability. Most gardeners use a combination of the two, but purely organic enthusiasts use natural products exclusively.

## Speaking the Language

Every fertilizer sold must have a label detailing its contents. Understanding the composition and numbers improves the gardener's ability to provide nutrition. The three numbers on a fertilizer label relate to its contents; the first number indicates the amount of nitrogen, the second number the amount of phosphorus, and the third the amount of potassium. For example, if the numbers are 20-15-10, it means the product has 20 percent nitrogen, 15 percent phosphorus, and 10 percent potassium. Their relative numbers reveal their impact on plants—a formula high in nitrogen greens-up the plant and grows leaves, ones with lower first and higher second and third numbers encourage flowers and fruits.

A good rule of thumb is to use a balanced fertilizer (one where all the numbers are equal, as in 10-10-10) to prepare new soil. Then fertilize the plants with a formula higher in nitrogen at the beginning of the growing season to get plants up and growing; switch to special formulas (that is, those formulated specifically for flowers and fruiting) later in the season.

Fertilizers can be water-soluble or granular; both types have advantages and appropriate uses. Soluble formulas are mixed in water. They are available in very specific formulas, compact to store, fast acting, and can be used either as a soil drench or to spray the leaves (plants will absorb them through foliage or soil). Solubles work quickly (leaves will often green up overnight—great if you want the yard to look good for a cookout), but their effects do not last long and they must be reapplied frequently. They are especially useful in growing container plants, which need more frequent watering as well as fertilizing.

Granular fertilizers can be worked into the soil when tilling or used as a top dressing around established plants. They incorporate easily into soils, and their effects may last for several weeks. Slow-release fertilizers, which are usually pelleted, keep working for three to nine months depending on the formula. The coated pellets of these popular fertilizers (with names like Osmocote, Polyon, and Once) decompose slowly with water or temperature changes over time. They cost more than granular fertilizers but save much time for the gardener because they're usually applied just once a season. Their other big advantage over granular fertilizers is that it's almost impossible for gardeners to "burn" plant foliage when using them; whereas, great care must be taken to keep granular fertilizers off plant parts.

Organic fertilizers also work very slowly, over a long period of time. They usually have lower ratios of active ingredients (nitrogen, phosphorus, and potassium) and so provide steady nutrition, rather than a quick green-up. Organic fertilizers that provide nitrogen are bloodmeal, fishmeal, soybean meal, and cottonseed meal. Organic phosphorous fertilizers include bonemeal and rock phosphate. To provide potassium, use greensand or sulfate of potash-magnesia.

Although soil may contain many nutrients, most gardeners find applying fertilizer makes growing plants more satisfactory. However, many tend to overdo it. Too much fertilizer can harm plants, just as too little does. Excessive nitrogen often leads to attacks of aphids, which appreciate the tender young growth that's being produced, and to floppy stems in perennial plants.

### Rules to Remember
* Never fertilize a dry plant. Water the day before you fertilize at least, or several hours before.
* Always use products at the recommended rate or a bit lower. Never use more than what is recommended.
* Rinse stray granules off plant leaves to prevent burning.

# Mulch

One important thing you can provide your plants—which may mean the difference between success and failure—is mulch.

## Mulch Matters

Mulch is the most useful material in your garden. A blanket of mulch keeps soil warmer in winter and cooler in summer, prevents erosion, and doesn't allow the soil surface to develop a hard crust. When heavy rain or drought causes water stress, mulch ameliorates both situations, acting as a barrier to flooding and conserving water in dry soil. Mulch suppresses weed growth and prevents soil from splashing onto leaves (and thus reduces the spread of soilborne diseases). A neat circle of mulch around newly planted trees offers a physical barrier to keep lawnmowers and string trimmers away from tender trunks. (Such trunk damage is one of the leading causes of death for young trees.) Mulch also makes a garden look neater than it does with just bare soil.

## What Mulch Is

Mulch can be any material, organic or inorganic, that covers the soil's surface. Popular organic mulches include hardwood barks (ground, shredded, or nuggets), pine and wheat straws, shredded leaves and leaf mold, and shredded newsprint and other papers. Your excess grass clippings also make a great mulch, provided you let them age a week or so (until they're no longer hot) before using, so they don't burn plants. Organic mulches gradually break down and enrich the soil.

If you can find a source of free organic material in your area—peanut hulls, ground-up corncobs, waste from an old cotton gin, or similar materials—so much the better. I have a friend who's a high school industrial arts teacher, and several times a year he brings me enormous bags of sawdust, left over from his students' projects. Some of it I let rot and use as a soil amendment, but I also spread quite a bit of the fresh sawdust around all sorts of plants as mulch.

And, of course, don't overlook rotted leaves as an excellent no-cost mulch. I've often wondered why some homeowners lug bags of leaves to the curb in fall, then, in spring, turn around and spend money to buy bags and bales of mulch material from a nursery.

Inorganic mulches can be made from pea gravel, crushed lava rock, marble chips, crushed pottery chards, and clear or black plastic. Also available in garden centers to be used as mulch are rolls of landscape fabric, which look like a thick cloth. Both plastic and landscape fabric need to be covered with a layer of an organic mulch for appearance's sake, unless used in the vegetable garden.

In general, organic mulches are best around your yard's ornamental plantings. Black plastic and some landscape fabrics can prevent air, water, and nutrients from readily reaching the roots of your plants. They also cause shallow root growth, which makes the plants more susceptible to drought.

Because pea gravel and other stone mulches are difficult to move if you decide you don't like the way they look, you may want to try them in a small spot first. They're ideal, however, for pathways and other permanent areas, because they don't rot or float away.

### What Can Mulch Do?

Beyond practical considerations, you may want to think about what different mulch materials offer the landscape aesthetically. The color and texture of many mulches can be attractive and offer contrast to green plants and lawns. Used on walkways and paths, mulch should provide a comfortable walking surface in addition to adding color and weed control to high-traffic areas. Mulch adds definition to planting areas and can be extended to neatly cover thinning lawn areas under trees. Mulch also works as a landscape-unifying element—use the same mulch material throughout the garden to tie diverse plantings together visually and to reduce maintenance at the same time.

### Mulch Dos and Don'ts

- Apply mulch 3 inches deep when planting new trees and shrubs.
- Replenish mulch around perennials each year when tending established beds in spring or fall. Apply pine straw to a depth of about 5 inches because it quickly settles.
- Use pine straw to mulch plantings on slopes or hills, where other mulches may be washed away in hard rains.
- Don't pile mulch against a plant's stem or trunk; that can cause damage. Instead, start spreading mulch about 2 inches away from the plant.
- Don't pile mounds of mulch around trees; it's not good for them.
- When setting out small bedding plants, you may find it easier to mulch the entire bed first—then dig individual holes—rather than to try to spread mulch evenly around tiny seedlings.
- Don't spread mulch over weed-infested ground, thinking it will kill the weeds. Generally, they'll pop right through. Instead, weed before mulching.
- Add to the organic mulch around each plant yearly—9 to 12 months after you originally mulched. Think of this mulch renewal not as a chore, but as a garden job that pays rich dividends.
- In fall always add more mulch around plants that may be damaged by an extra-cold winter.
- Wait until the soil has reliably warmed up (usually in May sometime) before mulching heat-loving plants, such as perennial hibiscus, caladium, and Madagascar periwinkle. If they're mulched too early, the soil will remain cool and they'll get off to a very slow start.
- Don't mulch ground that stays wet all the time.
- Don't over-do the mulch. More than 4 or 5 inches of mulch may prevent water from penetrating to the soil below.

# Glossary

**Alkaline soil:** soil with a pH greater than 7.0. It lacks acidity, often because it has limestone in it.

**All-purpose fertilizer:** powdered, liquid, or granular fertilizer with a balanced proportion of the three key nutrients—nitrogen (N), phosphorus (P), and potassium (K). It is suitable for maintenance nutrition for most plants.

**Annual:** a plant that lives its entire life in one season. It is genetically determined to germinate, grow, flower, set seed, and die the same year.

**Balled and burlapped:** describes a tree or shrub grown in the field whose soilball was wrapped with protective burlap and twine when the plant was dug up to be sold or transplanted.

**Bare root:** describes plants that have been packaged without any soil around their roots. (Often young shrubs and trees purchased through the mail arrive with their exposed roots covered with moist peat or sphagnum moss, sawdust, or similar material, and wrapped in plastic.)

**Barrier plant:** a plant that has intimidating thorns or spines and is sited purposely to block foot traffic or other access to the home or yard.

**Beneficial insects:** insects or their larvae that prey on pest organisms and their eggs. They may be flying insects, such as ladybugs, parasitic wasps, praying mantids, and soldier bugs, or soil dwellers such as predatory nematodes, spiders, and ants.

**Berm:** a narrow, raised ring of soil around a tree, used to hold water so it will be directed to the root zone.

**Bract:** a modified leaf structure on a plant stem near its flower, resembling a petal. Often it is more colorful and visible than the actual flower, as in dogwood.

**Bud union:** the place where the top of a plant was grafted to the rootstock; usually refers to roses.

**Canopy:** the overhead branching area of a tree, usually referring to its extent including foliage.

**Cold hardiness:** the ability of a perennial plant to survive the winter cold in a particular area.

**Composite:** a flower that is actually composed of many tiny flowers. Typically, they are flat clusters of tiny, tight florets, sometimes surrounded by wider-petaled florets. Composite flowers are highly attractive to bees and beneficial insects.

**Compost:** organic matter that has undergone progressive decomposition by microbial and macrobial activity until it is reduced to a spongy, fluffy texture. Added to soil of any type, it improves the soil's ability to hold air and water and to drain well.

**Corm:** the swollen energy-storing structure, analogous to a bulb, under the soil at the base of the stem of plants such as crocus and gladiolus.

**Crown:** the base of a plant at, or just beneath, the surface of the soil where the roots meet the stems.

**Cultivar:** a CULTIvated VARiety. It is a naturally occurring form of a plant that has been identified as special or superior and is purposely selected for propagation and production.

**Deadhead:** a pruning technique that removes faded flower heads from plants to improve their appearances, abort seed production, and stimulate further flowering.

**Deciduous plants:** unlike evergreens, these trees and shrubs lose their leaves in the fall.

**Desiccation:** drying out of foliage tissues, usually due to drought or wind.

**Division:** the practice of splitting apart perennial plants to create several smaller-rooted segments. The practice is useful for controlling the plant's size and for acquiring more plants; it is also essential to the health and continued flowering of certain ones.

**Dormancy:** the period, usually the winter, when perennial plants temporarily cease active growth and rest. Dormant is the verb form, as used in this sentence: *Some plants, like spring-blooming bulbs, go dormant in the summer.*

**Established:** the point at which a newly planted tree, shrub, or flower begins to produce new growth, either foliage or stems. This is an indication that the roots have recovered from transplant shock and have begun to grow and spread.

**Evergreen:** perennial plants that do not lose their foliage annually with the onset of winter. Needled or broadleaf foliage will persist and continues to function on a plant through one or more winters, aging and dropping unobtrusively in cycles of three or four years or more.

**Floret:** a tiny flower, usually one of many forming a cluster, that comprises a single blossom.

**Foliar:** of or about foliage—usually refers to the practice of spraying foliage, as in fertilizing or treating with insecticide; leaf tissues absorb liquid directly for fast results, and the soil is not affected.

**Germinate:** to sprout. Germination is a fertile seed's first stage of development.

**Graft (union):** the point on the stem of a woody plant with sturdier roots where a stem from a highly ornamental plant is inserted so that it will join with it. Roses are commonly grafted.

**Hands:** the female flowers on a banana tree; they turn into bananas.

**Hardscape:** the permanent, structural, nonplant part of a landscape, such as walls, sheds, pools, patios, arbors, and walkways.

**Herbaceous:** plants having fleshy or soft stems that die back with frost; the opposite of woody.

**Hybrid:** a plant that is the result of intentional or natural cross-pollination between two or more plants of the same species or genus.

**Low water demand:** describes plants that tolerate dry soil for varying periods of time. Typically, they have succulent, hairy, or silvery-gray foliage and tuberous roots or taproots.

**Mulch:** a layer of material over bare soil to protect it from erosion and compaction by rain, and to discourage weeds. It may be inorganic (gravel, fabric) or organic (wood chips, bark, pine needles, chopped leaves).

**Naturalize:** (*a*) to plant seeds, bulbs, or plants in a random, informal pattern as they would appear in their natural habitats; (*b*) to adapt to and spread throughout adopted habitats (a tendency of some nonnative plants).

**Nectar:** the sweet fluid produced by glands on flowers that attract pollinators such as hummingbirds and honeybees, for whom it is a source of energy.

**Organic material, organic matter:** any material or debris that is derived from plants. It is carbon-based material capable of undergoing decomposition and decay.

**Peat moss:** organic matter from peat sedges (United States) or sphagnum mosses (Canada), often used to improve soil texture. The acidity of sphagnum peat moss makes it ideal for boosting or maintaining soil acidity while also improving its drainage.

**Perennial:** a flowering plant that lives over two or more seasons. Many die back with frost, but their roots survive the winter and generate new shoots in the spring.

**pH:** a measurement of the relative acidity (low pH) or alkalinity (high pH) of soil or water based on a scale of 1 to 14, 7 being neutral. Individual plants require soil to be within a certain range so that nutrients can dissolve in moisture and be available to them.

**Pinch:** to remove tender stems and/or leaves by pressing them between thumb and forefinger. This pruning technique encourages branching, compactness, and flowering in plants, or it removes aphids clustered at growing tips.

**Pollen:** the yellow, powdery grains in the center of a flower. A plant's male sex cells, they are transferred to the female plant parts by means of wind or animal pollinators to fertilize them and create seeds.

**Raceme:** an arrangement of single-stalked flowers along an elongated, unbranched axis.

**Rhizome:** a swollen energy-storing stem structure, similar to a bulb, that lies horizontally in the soil, with roots emerging from its lower surface and growth shoots from a growing point at or near its tip, as in bearded iris.

**Rootbound (or potbound):** the condition of a plant that has been confined in a container too long, its roots having been forced to wrap around themselves and even swell out of the container. Successful transplanting or repotting requires untangling and trimming away of some of the matted roots.

**Root flare:** the transition at the base of a tree trunk where the bark tissue begins to differentiate and roots begin to form just before entering the soil. This area should not be covered with soil when planting a tree.

**Self-seeding:** the tendency of some plants to sow their seeds freely around the yard. It creates many seedlings the following season that may or may not be welcome.

**Semievergreen:** tending to be evergreen in a mild climate but deciduous in a rigorous one.

**Shearing:** the pruning technique whereby plant stems and branches are cut uniformly with long-bladed pruning shears (hedge shears) or powered hedge trimmers. It is used when creating and maintaining hedges and topiary.

**Slow-acting fertilizer:** fertilizer that is water insoluble and therefore releases its nutrients gradually as a function of soil temperature, moisture, and related microbial activity. Typically granular, it may be organic or synthetic.

**Succulent growth:** the sometimes undesirable production of fleshy, water-storing leaves or stems that results from overfertilization.

**Sucker:** a new-growing shoot. Underground plant roots produce suckers to form new stems and spread by means of these suckering roots to form large plantings, or colonies. Some plants produce root suckers or branch suckers as a result of pruning or wounding.

**Tuber:** a type of underground storage structure in a plant stem, analogous to a bulb. It generates roots below and stems above ground (example: dahlia).

**Variegated:** having various colors or color patterns. The term usually refers to plant foliage that is streaked, edged, blotched, or mottled with a contrasting color—often green with yellow, cream, or white.

**White grubs:** fat, off-white, wormlike larvae of Japanese beetles. They reside in the soil and feed on plant (especially grass) roots until summer when they emerge as beetles to feed on plant foliage.

**Wings:** (*a*) the corky tissue that forms edges along the twigs of some woody plants such as winged euonymus; (*b*) the flat, dried extension of tissue on some seeds, such as maple, that catch the wind and help them disseminate.

# Bibliography

## Reference Books

Armitage, Allan M. *Herbaceous Perennial Plants*. Champaign, Illinois: Stipes Publishing, 1997.

Bender, Steve, editor. *The Southern Living Garden Problem Solver*. Birmingham, Alabama: Oxmoor House, 1999.

Darke, Rick. *Color Encyclopedia of Ornamental Grasses*. Portland, Oregon: Timber Press, 1999.

Dirr, Michael A. *Manual of Woody Landscape Plants*. Champaign, Illinois: Stipes Publishing, 1998.

DiSabito-Aust, Tracy. *The Well-Tended Perennial Garden*. Portland, Oregon: Timber Press, 1998.

Heriteau, Jacqueline and Marc Cathey, editors. *The National Arboretum Book of Outstanding Garden Plants*. New York, New York: Simon & Schuster, 1990.

Hoshizaki, Barbara Joe and Robbin C. Moran. *Fern Grower's Manual*. Portland, Oregon: Timber Press, 2001.

## General Reading

Bender, Steve and Felder Rushing. *Passalong Plants*. Chapel Hill, North Carolina: The University of North Carolina Press, 1993.

Hodgson, Larry. *Perennials for Every Purpose*. Emmaus, Pennsylvania: Rodale Press, 2000.

Holmes, Roger, editor. *Taylor's Guide to Ornamental Grasses*. Boston, Massachusetts: Houghton Mifflin Co., 1997.

Ogden, Scott. *Garden Bulbs for the South*. Dallas, Texas: Taylor Publishing, 1994.

Roth, Susan A. *The Four-Season Landscape*. Emmaus, Pennsylvania: Rodale Press, 1994.

Sedenko, Jerry. *The Butterfly Garden*. New York, New York: Villard Books, 1991.

Xerces Society, The, and The Smithsonian Institution. *Butterfly Gardening*. San Francisco, California: Sierra Club Books, 1998.

# Photography Credits

# Plant Index

Acer
 griseum 68-69
  'Cinnamon Flake' 69
  'Gingerbread'™ 69
 palmatum 48-49
  'Bloodgood' 49
  'Red Dragon' 49
 rubrum 78-79
  'Autumn Blaze' 79
  'October Glory' 79
  'Red Sunset'® 79
 saccharum 94-95
  'Green Mountain'® 95
  'Legacy' 95
Allegheny serviceberry 89
Amelanchier
 arborea 89
 canadensis 89
 grandiflora 89
  'Autumn Brilliance' 89
  'Princess Diana' 89
 laevis 89
American Holly 12-13
 'Emily Bruner' 13
 'Fosteri' 13
 'James Swan' 13
 'Jersey Knight' 13
 'Jersey Princess' 13
 'Nellie R. Stevens' 13
American Hornbeam 14-15
Astilbe 23
Azalea 23, 25, 39, 51, 97
Bald Cypress 16-17
 'Apache Chief' 17
Barberry 75
Betula nigra 82-83
 'Heritage' 83
Black Gum 18-19
 'Jermyn's Flame' 19
Blue Atlas Cedar 20-21
 'Argentea' 21
 'Aurea' 21
 'Glauca Pendula' 21
Bougainvillea Golden
 Rain Tree 45
Canadian
 Hemlock 9, 22-23
  'Golden Splendor' 23
  'Sargentii' 23
Cardinal Flower 23
Carolina Silverbell 24-25
 'Arnold Pink' 25
 'Rosea' 25

Carpinus caroliniana 14-15
Cedar
 Blue Atlas 20-21
  'Argentea' 21
  'Aurea' 21
  'Glauca Pendula' 21
 Deodar 34-35
  'Shalimar' 35
Cedrus
 atlantica 20
  'Argentea' 21
  'Aurea' 21
  'Glauca' 21
  'Glauca Pendula' 21
 deodara 34-35
  'Shalimar' 35
Cercidiphyllum japonicum 54-55
 'Pendula' 55
Cercis canadensis 76-77
 'Forest Pansy' 77
 'Royal White' 77
 'Tennessee Pink' 77
Chaste Tree 26-27
 'Blushing Spires' 27
 'Silver Spire' 27
Cherry
 'Amanogawa' 59
 Kwanzan 58-59
 'Royal Burgundy 59'
 Yoshino 110-111
  'Cascade Snow'™ 111
  'Royal Burgundy' 111
Chinese Fringe Tree 41
Chinese Pistachio 28-29
Chinese Stewartia 51
Chionanthus
 retusus 41
 virginicus 40-41
Cladastris kentukea 108-109
 'Rosea' 109
Cornelian Cherry 30-31
 'Golden Glory' 31
 'Variegata' 31
Cornus
 florida 38-39
  'Big Apple' 39
  'Cherokee Princess' 39
 kousa 56-57
  'Moonbeam' 57
  var. chinensis 'Milky
   Way' 57
 mas 30-31
  'Golden Glory' 31

 'Variegata' 31
Crabapple
 Flowering 36-37
  'Callaway' 37
  'Centurion' 37
  'Donald Wyman' 37
  Japanese 37
  'Prairiefire' 37
Crataegus
 phaenopyrum 107
 viridis 'Winter King' 106-107
Cryptomeria japonica 46-47
 'Benjamin Franklin' 47
 'Gyokuryu' 47
Cupressaceae x
 cupressocyparis
 leylandii 62-63
  'Castlewellan Gold'® 63
  'Irish Mint' 63
  'Monca' 63
  'Naylor's Blue' 63
Daffodil 39
Dawn Redwood 32-33
Deodar Cedar 34-35
 'Shalimar' 35
Dogwood 77, 101
 Flowering 38-39
  'Big Apple' 39
  'Cherokee Princess' 39
 Kousa 38, 39, 56-57
  'Moonbeam' 57
  var. chinensis 'Milky
   Way' 57
Evergreen Trees
 American Holly 12-13
 Blue Atlas Cedar 20-21
 Canadian Hemlock 22-23
 Deodar Cedar 34-35
 Japanese Cryptomeria 46-47
 Leyland Cypress 62-63
 Norway Spruce 64-65
 Southern Magnolia 92-93
 Sweet Bay
  Magnolia 96-97
Fern 23
Flowering Crabapple 36-37
 'Callaway' 37
 'Centurion' 37
 'Donald Wyman' 37
 Japanese 37
 'Prairiefire' 37
Flowering Dogwood 38-39
 'Big Apple' 39

'Cherokee Princess' 39
Flowering Trees
  Carolina Silverbell 24-25
  Chaste Tree 26-27
  Cornelian Cherry 30-31
  Flowering Crabapple 36-37
  Flowering Dogwood 38-39
  Fringe Tree 40-41
  Golden Rain Tree 44-45
  Japanese Stewartia 50-51
  Kousa Dogwood 56-57
  Kwanzan Cherry 58-59
  Ornamental Pear 66-67
  Purple Leaf Plum 74-75
  Redbud 76-77
  Saucer Magnolia 86-87
  Serviceberry 88-89
  Southern Magnolia 92-93
  Sweet Bay
    Magnolia 96-97
  Tulip Poplar 102-103
  Winter King
    Hawthorn 106-107
  Yellowwood 108-109
  Yoshino Cherry 110-111
Fothergilla 71
Fringe Tree 40-41
*Ginkgo biloba* 42-43
  'Autumn Gold'™ 43
  'Shangri-La'® 43
*Gleditsia triacanthos f.*
  *inermis* 100-101
    'Halka'™ 101
    'Moraine' 101
    'Shademaster'® 101
    'Sunburst' 101
Golden Rain Tree 44-45
  Bougainvillea 45
*Halesia tetraptera* 24-25
  'Arnold Pink' 25
  'Rosea' 25
Hawthorn
  Washington 107
  Winter King 106-107
Holly
  American 12-13
Hornbeam
  American 14-15
Hosta 23
*Ilex opaca* 12-13
  'Emily Bruner' 13
  'Fosteri' 13
  'James Swan' 13
  'Jersey Knight' 13
  'Jersey Princess' 13
  'Nellie R. Stevens' 13

Japanese Cryptomeria 46-47
  'Benjamin Franklin' 47
  'Gyokuryu' 47
Japanese Maple 48-49
  'Bloodgood' 49
  'Red Dragon' 49
Japanese Stewartia 50-51
Japanese Zelkova 52-53
  'Green Vase'® 53
Katsura Tree 54-55
  'Pendula' 55
*Koelreuteria*
  *bipinnata* 45
  *paniculata* 44-45
Korean stewartia 51
Kousa Dogwood 38, 39,
  56-57
  'Moonbeam' 57
  var. *chinensis* 'Milky
    Way' 57
Kwanzan Cherry 58-59
Lacebark Elm 60-61
  'Dynasty' 61
  'Golden Rey' 61
Leyland Cypress 62-63
  'Castlewellan Gold'® 63
  'Irish Mint' 63
  'Monca' 63
  'Naylor's Blue' 63
Lily-of-the-Valley 25
*Liquidambar*
  *styraciflua* 98-99
    'Cherokee'® 99
    'Palo Alto' 99
    'Rotundiloba' 99
*Liriodendron*
  *tulipifera* 102-103
    'Ardis' 103
    'Compactum' 103
Loropetalum 75
*Magnolia*
  *grandiflora* 92-93
    'Bracken's Brown
      Beauty' 93
    'Edith Bogue' 93
    'Little Gem' 93
    'Riegel' 93
    'Spring Hill' 93
  *virginiana* 96-97
  x *soulangiana* 86-87
    'Alba' 87
    'Rustica Rubra' 87
*Malus* 36-37
  'Callaway' 37
  'Centurion' 37
  'Donald Wyman' 37

  *floribunda* 37
  'Indian Summer' 37
Maple 9
  Japanese 48-49
    'Bloodgood' 49
    'Red Dragon' 49
  Paperbark 68-69
    'Cinnamon Flake' 69
    'Gingerbread'™ 69
  Red 78-79
    'Autumn Blaze' 79
    'October Glory' 79
    'Red Sunset'® 79
  Sugar 94-95
    'Green Mountain'® 95
    'Legacy' 95
*Metasequoia*
  *glyptostroboides* 32-33
Mountain Laurel 23
Norway Spruce 64-65
  'Cupressina' 65
*Nyssa sylvatica* 18-19
  'Jermyn's Flame' 19
Oak
  Pin 72-73
    'Sovereign' 73
  Red 80-81
  White 81
  Willow 104-105
Oakleaf Hydrangea 23
Ornamental Pear 66-67
  'Bradford' 66, 67
  'Chanticleer'® 67
  'Edgewood' 67
  'Fauriei' 67
  'Korean Sun'® 67
*Oxydendrum arboretum* 90-91
  'Chameleon' 91
Paperbark Maple 68-69
  'Cinnamon Flake' 69
  'Gingerbread'™ 69
*Parrotia persica* 70-71
  'Pendula' 71
Pear
  Ornamental 66-67
    'Bradford' 66, 67
    'Chanticleer'® 67
    'Edgewood' 67
    'Fauriei' 67
    'Korean Sun'® 67
Persian Ironwood 70-71
  'Pendula' 71
*Picea abies* 64-65
  'Cupressina' 65
Pin Oak 72-73
  'Sovereign' 73

*Pistacia chinensis* 28-29
*Prunus*
  *cerasifera* 74-75
    'Atropurpurea' 75
    'Hollywood' 75
    'Purpusii' 75
  *serrulata*
    'Amanogawa' 59
    'Kwanzan' 58-59
    'Royal Burgundy' 59
  x *yedoensis* 110-111
    'Cascade Snow'™ 111
    'Royal Burgundy' 111
Purple Leaf Plum 74-75
  'Atropurpurea' 75
  'Hollywood' 75
  'Purpusii' 75
*Pyrus calleryana* 66-67
  'Bradford' 66, 67
  'Chanticleer'® 67
  'Edgewood' 67
  'Fauriei' 67
  'Korean Sun'® 67
*Quercus*
  *alba* 81
  *palustris* 72-73
    'Sovereign' 73
  *phellos* 104-105
  *rubra* 80-81
Red Maple 78-79
  'Autumn Blaze' 79
  'October Glory' 79
  'Red Sunset'® 79
Red Oak 80-81
Redbud 76-77
  'Forest Pansy' 77
  'Royal White' 77
  'Tennessee Pink' 77
River Birch 82-83
  'Heritage' 83
Rhododendron 23, 25, 111
*Sassafras albidum* 84-85
Saucer Magnolia 86-87
  'Alba' 87

'Rustica Rubra' 87
Serviceberry 88-89
  'Autumn Brilliance' 89
  'Princess Diana' 89
Shadbush 89
Shade Trees
  American Hornbeam 14-15
  Chinese Pistachio 28-29
  Gingko 42-43
  Japanese Maple 48-49
  Japanese Zelkova 52-53
  Katsura 54-55
  Lacebark Elm 60-61
  Paperbark Maple 68-69
  Persian Ironwood 70-71
  Pin Oak 72-73
  Red Maple 78-79
  Red Oak 80-81
  River Birch 82-83
  Sassafras 84-85
  Sourwood 90-91
  Sugar Maple 94-95
  Sweet Gum 98-99
  Thornless Honey
    Locust 100-101
  Tulip Poplar 102-103
  Willow Oak 104-105
  Yellowwood 108-109
Sourwood 90-91
  'Chameleon' 91
Southern Magnolia 9, 92-93
  'Bracken's Brown
    Beauty' 93
  'Edith Bogue' 93
  'Little Gem' 93
  'Riegel' 93
  'Spring Hill' 93
*Stewartia*
  Chinese 51
  Japanese 50-51
  Korean 51
  *koreana* 51
  *pseudocamellia* 50-51
  *sinensis* 51

Sugar Maple 94-95
  'Green Mountain'® 95
  'Legacy' 95
Swamp Magnolia 97
Sweet Bay Magnolia 96-97
Sweet Gum 11, 98-99
  'Cherokee'® 99
  'Palo Alto' 99
  'Rotundiloba' 99
*Taxodium distichum* 16-17
  'Apache Chief' 17
Thornless Honey
  Locust 100-101
    'Halka'™ 101
    ' 101
    'Shademaster'® 101
    'Sunburst' 101
*Tsuga canadensis* 22-23
  'Golden Splendor' 23
  'Sargentii' 23
Tulip 39
Tulip Poplar 102-103
  'Ardis' 103
  'Compactum' 103
*Ulmus parvifolia* 60-61
  'Dynasty' 61
  'Golden Rey' 61
*Vitex agnus-castus* 26-27
  'Blushing Spires' 27
  'Silver Spire' 27
Washington Hawthorn 107
White Oak 81
Willow Oak 104-105
Winter hazel 71
Winter King Hawthorn 106-107
Witchhazel 65, 71
Yellowwood 108-109
  'Rosea' 109
Yoshino Cherry 110-111
    'Cascade Snow'™ 111
    'Royal Burgundy' 111
*Zelkova serrata* 52-53
  'Green Vase'® 53

# Want to know more about Tennessee gardening?

*Interested in fantastic flowers for Tennessee? Do you want healthful, tasty herbs, fruits, and vegetables from your Tennessee garden? How about stunning Tennessee shrubs?*

If you enjoy *50 Great Trees for Tennessee*, you will appreciate similar books featuring Tennessee flowers, vegetables (including fruits and herbs), and shrubs. These valuable books also deserve a place in your gardening library.

## 50 Great Flowers for Tennessee

Judy Lowe shares her personal recommendations on fifty delightful flowering plants for Tennessee. From colorful annuals that give you spring-to-fall color, to hard-working perennials that return year after year, you will find much to choose from in this book.

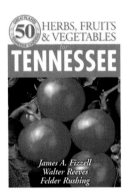

## 50 Great Herbs, Fruits and Vegetables for Tennessee

If you are inclined to "edibles" in your Tennessee garden, this is the book for you. It provides valuable advice on how to select, plant, and grow tasty herbs, luscious fruits, and flavorful vegetables. Written by James A. Fizzell, Walter Reeves, and Felder Rushing, this book offers more than seventy-five years of gardening wisdom all in an easy-to-use format.

## 50 Great Shrubs for Tennessee

If you want guidance on great shrubs for Tennessee, this is the book for you. From the boxwood to the flowering azalea, Judy Lowe shares her gardening wit and wisdom on fifty wonderful shrubs for Tennessee.

**Look for each of these books today.**